SCHOOL OF ORIENTAL AND AFRICAN STUDIES
University of London

Please return this book on or before the last date shown

Long loans and One Week loans may be renewed up to 10 times
Short loans & CDs cannot be renewed
Fines are charged on all overdue items

Online: http://lib.soas.ac.uk/patroninfo
Phone: 020-7898 4197 (answe~

2 3 OCT 2007

2 8 APR 2008

1 9 APR 2010

SOAS LIBRARY
WITHDRAWN

SOAS

1903925720

627337

China Through Western Eyes

The Nineteenth Century

A READER IN HISTORY

J.A.G. Roberts

Principal Lecturer in History
The Polytechnic of Huddersfield

ALAN SUTTON

For Jan

First Published in the United Kingdom in 1991 by
Alan Sutton Publishing Limited
Phoenix Mill · Far Thrupp · Stroud · Gloucestershire

First Published in the United States of America in 1992 by
Alan Sutton Publishing Inc · Wolfeboro Falls · NH · 03896–0848

Copyright © J.A.G. Roberts, 1991

All rights reserved. No part of this publication may be reproduced,
stored in a retrieval system, or transmitted, in any form, or by any
means, electronic, mechanical, photocopying, recording or otherwise,
without the prior permission of the publishers and copyright holders.

British Library Cataloguing in Publication Data

Roberts, J.A.G. (John Anthony George), *1935–*
China through Western eyes : the nineteenth century.
I. Title
951

ISBN 086299 828 X

Library of Congress Cataloguing in Publication data applied for

Cover picture: 'What we ought to do in China', from *Punch*,
22 December 1860.

Typeset in 10/12 Ehrhardt.
Typesetting and origination by
Alan Sutton Publishing Limited.
Printed in Great Britain by
The Bath Press, Bath, Avon.

CONTENTS

INTRODUCTION: WESTERN SOURCES ON CHINA IN THE NINETEENTH CENTURY

In the eighteenth century, European admiration for China reached remarkable heights. The *philosophes* of the Enlightenment, basing their opinions on reports from Jesuit missionaries, led the way in expressing this view. Voltaire said of the Chinese political system, 'the human spirit cannot imagine a better government'. The *philosophes* enthused particularly about the religious toleration which they believed was practised in China. They also extolled Chinese manufactures, especially porcelain, and this was reflected in the vogue for chinoiserie in the mid-eighteenth century.

This admiration was echoed in Great Britain, but to a lesser degree, and was matched by hostile references. In *The Farther Adventures of Robinson Crusoe*, published in 1719, Daniel Defoe described the Chinese as a 'miserable people'. British dealings with China were predominantly commercial, and the frustration experienced when dealing with officials tarnished the image of the Chinese. Lord Anson visited Canton in the course of his circumnavigation of the world in 1740–4. His chaplain was struck by the 'artifices, extortions, and frauds' practised by the Chinese on the visitors.

Towards the end of the century, when the focus of attention had shifted to the revolutionary struggle in Europe, a new chapter in the West's relationship with China began. With the onset of the industrial revolution, Britain's need to expand her overseas markets became

1

apparent. One obvious target was China, believed to have an enormous commercial potential, but where trade, since 1760, had been restricted to the single southern port of Canton. In 1792 the Earl of Macartney headed an embassy to China, the chief objectives of which were to establish diplomatic relations and to obtain access to other ports. The total failure of the mission ensured that China would eventually be forced to revise her relationship with the West.

Under these circumstances it was not surprising that the dominant view of China held by westerners changed. In the place of Voltaire, one might quote the Revd John Gray, Archdeacon of Canton, a man generally well-disposed towards the Chinese, who wrote: 'Their religion is a mass of superstitions. Their government is, in form, that which of all others is perhaps most liable to abuse – an irresponsible despotism.'[1]

From the time of the Macartney mission the number of merchants, missionaries, diplomats and travellers going to China began to increase. Their writings are the material of this book. The literature which they produced was substantial, especially if official records, newspapers and unpublished sources are included. This Reader does not survey it all: its emphasis is on the sources which are more readily available, which implies works which have appeared in print and in English. Particular use has been made of books which have been reprinted in recent years. Nevertheless the amount of material is very large and a number of criteria have been used in selecting the extracts.

Most of the passages chosen were based on the first-hand experience of the writer who may have played a notable role in the events described, or who could claim expertise on the matter discussed. Some space has been reserved for those whose opinion of the Chinese was based not on knowledge of the race, but of its products. The contributor to the *Edinburgh Review* of the review of Sir George Staunton's book on the penal code of China, justified such comment by saying:

The representations of travellers, even where their fidelity is liable to no impeachment, will almost always take a tinge from their own imagination or affections; and, where enthusiasm or controversy have any place in the discussion, there is an end to all prospect of accuracy or justice. The laws of a people, however, are actual specimens of their intellect and character . . .[2]

Most of the passages come from works written expressly for publication, but some extracts from journals and letters have been used, and these offer more private reflections on the Chinese. Robert Hart, who became Inspector General of the Imperial Maritime Customs, kept a private journal, part of which he later destroyed. Other keepers of journals included Lord Macartney, the Earl of Elgin and Charles Gordon, commander of the Ever-Victorious Army. As an example of a letter-writer there is the Revd John Kenneth Mackenzie who wrote home every fortnight. His attempt to describe China to relatives who had no experience of the country gave an added dimension to his writing.

Western sources may be said to contain valuable information both about China and about western attitudes towards that country and its people in the nineteenth century. The question arises – what is valuable in this context? The views of foreign observers may be more objective than those of indigenous writers. On the other hand, foreign observers may be inadequately trained or may be unreliable witnesses. As if in response to this accusation, many writers were at pains to define their credentials.

Whose opinion was most worthy of notice? For those who had lived for years on the China coast, there was no doubt that length of service was a an important criterion. Many writers prefaced their work with their claim in this respect. The Revd William Milne had spent 'fourteen years among the Chinese', J.R. Scarth called his book *Twelve Years in China*, the Revd R.H. Cobbold gave his qualifications as eight years among the Chinese at the port of Ningpo 'with frequent opportunities of travel in the province of Chekeang'.[3]

A particular claim to expertise came from those who had learned Chinese: there was no doubt in their minds that it was they who were best able to convey what was really happening in China. Rutherford Alcock argued the importance of training interpreters for the consular service, saying that '*five years' steady training*, added to an original aptitude for the acquisition of languages', was necessary to make a 'decent interpreter'. He had this to say about a writer who launched himself into print with no knowledge of the Chinese language:

... we see a new book noticed by the public press – 'Impressions of China and the present Revolution, its Progress and Prospects', by Captain Fishbourne, the Commander of the *Hermes*, which took Sir John Bonham when he made his trip to Nanking, then in possession of the insurgents. We shall hope to see this work before we conclude, but in the meantime ... we judge that it forms a very perfect antithesis to our argument, and must furnish the interpreters with an amusing instance of the mischief of not learning the language – of the fallacy of any man hoping to give a true impression of what he only imperfectly understands; but more especially it must shew into what a bottomless sea of errors and mistakes a foreigner, governed by a fixed idea, must inevitably fall, who, with no knowledge either of the people or their language, sits down to write a book on 'China – its Revolution, Progress and Prospects'. At the same time we are bound to add our conviction that no familiarity with the Chinese language would in this instance have been of the least avail to put the gallant Captain right, or in any way have applied a corrective to what the *Spectator* terms 'the groundless hopes, and headlong reasonings of a sanguine man engaged in riding a hobby'.[4]

Captain Fishbourne had worked in China, and was better qualified to write on the progress of rebellion than several others who ventured into print. Neither Charles Macfarlane, author of *The Chinese Revolution*, nor J. Milton Mackie, author of *Life of Taiping-wang* could claim first-hand knowledge. In its place they drew attention to their status as professional writers: on their title pages they identified themselves as 'Author of "Japan", "Life of Wellington",' etc., and 'Author of "Cosas de España", "Life of Schamyl",' etc. Their books were scissors-and-paste exercises, but because they preserved a number of early translations of documents they continue to be of some value.

However, compared with Captain Fishbourne, other westerners did seem better qualified. Rutherford Alcock spent twelve years in various consular offices in China before being appointed Consul-General in Japan. He returned to China as British ambassador in 1865, and eventually retired after twenty-seven years service in Asia. An even more notable example of the old China hand was Harry Parkes, who had begun his career as an interpreter and became one of whom *The Times'* journalist George Wingrove Cooke described as 'these twenty-years-in-the-country-and-speak-the-language men'.[5]

A real expert on China was the British interpreter Thomas Taylor Meadows who began to study Chinese in 1841 at the Royal University of Munich, and who took up the post of interpreter at the Canton consulate in 1843. Four years later he published his first book, *Desultory Notes on the Government and People of China*, in which he defined his qualifications:

> That the reader may be enabled to form some judgment as to the degree of reliance to be placed on the statements and opinions put forward in the following Notes, I shall here shew on what grounds I found my title to write on China.
>
> I conceive myself entitled to write on China, firstly, because I have some practical knowledge of the Chinese language; secondly, because I have bestowed my whole time and undivided attention on Chinese affairs for nearly five years; and thirdly, because, during nearly three years of that period, I have been placed in an unusually favourable position for acquiring a knowledge of those particular subjects on which I have ventured to write.[6]

Meadows was of a combative temperament. In his best-known book, *The Chinese and Their Rebellions*, he devoted a chapter to a review of *L'Empire Chinois* by the French missionary Évariste Huc. Meadows accepted that Huc had a knowledge of the Chinese language, and that he had travelled exceptionally widely in China, at a time when access to the interior was still forbidden. Nevertheless he charged the missionary with making or reproducing numerous errors in his work. The reason for this, said Meadows, was that Huc had quoted uncritically from the writings of French sinologues who had never been to China, and had obtained information from Chinese Christian converts, whose religion cut them off from other Chinese. Even when Huc was recounting his own experiences, Meadows argued that he was prone to exaggerate, claiming inaccurately that he had had constant dealings with Chinese high society. Huc had also implied that his knowledge of the interior of China gave his opinions special weight. Meadows, who had not travelled away from the coast, sought to disprove the 'interior of the country' claim, by pointing to the extensive opportunities for communicating with Chinese which were available to interpreters, such as himself, who resided in the treaty ports.[7]

The most weighty judgements on China and the Chinese were passed by officials and missionaries. Nevertheless there was room for other perspectives. J.R. Scarth prefaced his book *Twelve Years in China* with a thumbnail sketch of the tendencies of such persons when reporting on the Chinese scene, and continued with a plea for the recognition of a merchant viewpoint:

Most of the books upon China have been written by men of official position – by missionaries and by persons who have seen but little of the natives in daily general intercourse: the official stands upon his dignity and goes through the tedious forms of stiff diplomatic visits now and then; most of his information is derived from people who are devoted to the mandarins; the missionary has better opportunities, mixes more with the people, and his informants are less connected with the ruling authorities, but, from his position, he sees the Chinese in a different light to most other observers.[8]

The debate did not end there. S. Wells Williams, the well-known American missionary, claimed precedence for missionaries in passing judgment on the Chinese character in terms of 'falsity' and 'base ingratitude', arguing that ambassadors and merchants were less able to ascertain the moral character of the Chinese.

With the arrival of the special correspondent and the tourist, qualifications in terms of breadth rather than depth of experience became relevant. The first special correspondent to China, George Wingrove Cooke of *The Times*, enjoyed a reputation of being an influential moulder of opinion, and was bold enough to be sceptical about the views of China experts. But special correspondents, too, had to justify their authority. Archibald Colquhoun, also special correspondent of *The Times*, in the preface of his book *China in Transformation*, went to great pains to impress on his reader that it was the *variety* of his experience which made his opinions worthy of note:

Many years of service in Burma, first as an engineer, and later as Deputy-Commissioner; repeated visits to Siam, the latter on a Government mission and in a private capacity; prolonged stays in China as explorer, special correspondent of *The Times*, and, recently, in connection with important negotiations concerning railway questions – such, briefly, have been my qualifications in the Far East. Nor has my experience been limited to Eastern Asia. As the first Administrator of Mashonaland, where I had to deal with the work of colony-making, and on a special mission to examine the Nicaragua Canal scheme, and in visits to the United States and Canada, I may claim . . . to have prepared myself for forming a judgment upon the events which are passing in the Far East; for a writer on the Far Eastern problem should also have made a study of the West.[9]

Tourists claimed an audience because they also had been to many other parts of the world and could make comparisons. A good example of this genre was Henry M. Field's *From Egypt to Japan*. His description of a one-year tour of the world included a chapter on China. First published in 1877, by 1890 it had reached its sixteenth edition.

An important consideration in determining the value of a writer's contribution lay in the matter of access. Until the Treaty of Nanking in 1842, access to China was extremely limited. Canton was the only port open to foreign trade and westerners who travelled further did so surreptitiously. After 1842 foreigners had the right to venture half a day's journey from the five treaty ports, but had to return to their base by nightfall. In 1848, J.R. Scarth flouted this regulation and departed from Shanghai in disguise:

My object being to see the country as well as could be without interruption, and to penetrate as far as possible into the silk districts, I adopted the Chinese dress, and after getting fairly under way, metamorphosed myself into a Chinaman, set the barber to work to make a clean sweep of my hair, and, attached to my cap, wore a thorough-bred tail of some son of Han, shaded the natural colour of my barbarian eyes by a huge pair of tea-stone spectacles, and marched forth without fear of recognition.[10]

Scarth, like many other westerners, found that even when it was possible to travel in the interior, the Chinese response to the arrival of a foreigner, a mixture of curiosity and hostility, made it very difficult to make contact with individuals. He discovered that a 'sketch-book is the best weapon to travel with in China', because it provided people with a reason for one's wandering about, and kept them in good humour. In particular it made it easier to approach women and children. Thomas Taylor Meadows, who was six feet one inch tall, could not walk around undetected, so he had a duck-shooting boat specially adapted to enable him to make an excursion along the Grand Canal and to make contact with the Taiping rebels. Later in the nineteenth century, even when foreigners had the right to travel in the interior, they still used Chinese dress. T.T. Cooper journeyed up the Yangtze in 'pigtail and pet-ticoats', to avoid hostile incidents, and Archibald Colquhoun took 'full Chinese costume' with him on his journey through south China in 1882, to escape the curiosity of Chinese crowds.

As suggested above, foreign observers' objectivity could give a particular value to their descriptions. Objectivity, however, is a rare quality. Most writers had an axe to grind and some admitted this openly. Henry Sirr, in *China and the Chinese*, stated that a prime motivation for his writing was to attack the choice of Hong Kong as Britain's island base. With a certain lack of prescience, he began with a chapter entitled 'Hong Kong – Insalubrity and worthlessness'. A.F. Lindley also wore his heart on his sleeve. In the preface to his history of the Taiping revolution he stated: 'In writing this work I have been prompted by feelings of sympathy for a worthy, oppressed, and cruelly-wronged people; as well as a desire to protest against the evil foreign policy which England, during the last few years, has pursued towards *weak* Powers, especially in Asia.'[11]

Perhaps because they realized that the Chinese society they were observing could not survive, some westerners had a compulsive urge to record their experiences. An extreme example was the case of Dr Lamprey, the surgeon of the 67th Regiment. In 1864, in a town near Soochow, he saw a crowd looking at the head of a Chinese soldier who had just been decapitated for highway robbery. The doctor made a detailed record, in words and in a sketch, of the muscular spasms which the head continued to make over a period of ten minutes.[12] The same determination led T.T. Meadows to watch a man suffering death by slicing and Henry M. Field to observe the use of judicial torture.

With the appearance of the camera, the possibility of presenting China in a more precise manner became available. The *Arrow* war was one of the first occasions when photography was used on the battlefield and between 1868 and 1872 John Thompson took the photographs for *Illustrations of China and Its People*, which broke new ground in social documentation. But until the end of the century, though fine photographs were taken, photography remained a slow and cumbersome method of recording an impression. The production of printing plates from photographs was not generally adopted until the 1890s and travel books such as Archibald Colquhoun's *Across Chrysê*, published in 1883, were still illustrated with woodcuts taken from photographs. Until nearly the end of the century observers relied on the written word and on the sketch-book to record most of what they saw.

Most western accounts of China in the nineteenth century refer to the treaty ports and to the coastal regions. Even in 1871, T.T. Cooper could write: 'the great provinces of the interior have been scarcely visited, and the life and condition of the majority of its millions but superficially observed'. When they travelled in the interior of China, westerners met Chinese who were not affected by the xenophobia common in the treaty ports. These encounters often produced a very different impression. To quote Cooper again:

And an Englishman, who has lived among them as one of themselves, may venture to tell his countrymen that to know the Chinese middle-classes and the peasantry is to like them. Kindly, courteous, yet impulsive, they are as easily moved to friendship as we now deem them readily excited to barbarous outrage. Their very faults excite pity rather than anger; and it has often occurred to me that the most barbarous Chinese treatment of strangers in the present day is no worse than the reception given to strangers and foreigners not so long ago in our own land.[13]

As the range of western observation was extended, the more percipient writers recognized a problem which had been obvious all along: that of generalizing about the Chinese. Robert Hart wrote in his journal:

Writers in writing of China and the Chinese have in most instances fallen into the error of generalization unsupported by premises. *Ex uno disce omnes* is applicable in many matters: but given one particular Chinese – one particular spot of Chinese ground, from neither of these can one say what ought to be the character of customs in another part of the Empire, or what ought to be the habits of individuals in another Province.[14]

Hart said that when he used the word Chinese 'I refer to China more particularly from a *Ningpo* point of view.' A similar limitation can be found in a number of books published at that time.

The Revd Justus Doolittle's *Social Life of the Chinese* was subtitled *With Special but not Exclusive Reference to Fuhchau*, while the Revd M. Simpson Culbertson pointed out in the introduction to *Darkness in the Flowery Land*, that although much of what he had to say was applicable to the whole country, 'there is also much that is true only of the district about Ningpo and Shanghae'.

A discussion of the value of western accounts raises many other issues which cannot be dealt with in a brief introduction. But reference should be made to the use of language and to the expression of attitudes which today may be regarded as reprehensible. In the nineteenth century, assumptions of racial superiority among westerners were so deeply ingrained that few writings of the time were free from injurious remarks about other races. It is not the purpose of this Reader to encourage a revival of such attitudes and an attempt has been made to balance the offensive with the reflective comment.

Particular emphasis has been placed on extracts in which the writer puts his or her observation into a comparative context. The point of comparison is in itself interesting. Some writers, seeking to classify their experience in China, made comparisons with the classical world. Others drew parallels with the contemporary societies of colonial India, or of Ireland. But the most frequent comparison was with England and this was not always at China's expense. These comparisons offer some of the most perceptive views of China, and also give an insight into the attitudes and values of the writer.

The passages are arranged thematically, and each theme has a short introduction which identifies the writers and the main issues. To fully annotate each of the passages chosen would take many pages, and the reader has been left to pursue other references as desired.

NOTES

1. J.H. Gray, *China: A History of the Laws, Manners and Customs of the People*, 2 vols., London, 1878, I, 16.
2. 'Ta Tsing Leu Lee', *Edinburgh Review*, 16, 1810, p. 477.
3. R.H. Cobbold, *Pictures of the Chinese*, London, 1860, p. iii.
4. Rutherford Alcock, 'The Chinese Empire and Its Destinies', *Bombay Quarterly Review*, 4, October, 1855, p. 229.
5. G. Wingrove Cooke, *China: Being* The Times *Special Correspondence from China in the Years 1857–58*, London, 1858, p. 392.
6. T.T. Meadows, *Desultory Notes on the Government and People of China*, London, 1847, p. vii.
7. T.T. Meadows, *The Chinese and Their Rebellions*, London, 1856, pp. 51–73.
8. J.R. Scarth, *Twelve Years in China: The People, the Rebels, and the Mandarins*, Edinburgh, 1860, pp. 1–2.
9. Archibald R. Colquhoun, *China in Transformation*, London, 1898, pp. vi–vii.
10. Scarth, *op. cit.*, p. 5.
11. A.F. Lindley, *Ti-ping Tien-kwoh*, London, 1866, pp. vii–viii.
12. J. Lamprey, 'The Economy of the Chinese Army', *Journal of the Royal United Service Institution*, 11.46, 1867, pp. 420–1. A copy of the sketch is shown in Plate XXIII.
13. T.T. Cooper, *Travels of a Pioneer of Commerce in Pigtail and Petticoats*, London, 1871, pp. 2–3.
14. Robert Hart, *Entering China's Service*, London, 1986, p. 143.

THE MACARTNEY MISSION: CHINA BEFORE THE TREATIES

At the beginning of the nineteenth century, Western contacts with China were restricted to Canton, to the Russian Orthodox mission in Peking, and to the observations of a few hardy missionaries and explorers who risked punishment and travelled to the interior of China. As trade grew, the situation at Canton became increasingly irksome and private traders began to challenge the monopoly of the East India Company. The most important single commodity of the trade was tea. When, in 1784, William Pitt reduced the import duty on tea from over 100 per cent to 12.5 per cent, consumption of tea leapt and pressure to increase China's importation of British manufactured goods rose. It was agreed that to improve the trading relationship with China, proper diplomatic relations should be established and this led to the despatch of Macartney's embassy in 1792.

Macartney went to Peking, travelled beyond the Great Wall to Jehol, the summer capital, and returned by the Grand Canal and by river to Canton, altogether spending seven months in China. He was accompanied by experts in several fields, including medicine and botany, and by a Chinese interpreter. His embassy was undoubtedly the best-prepared expedition ever sent to China from the West and its records provide a detailed source of information on China at that time.

Macartney was sensitive to the attitude of the Chinese officials he encountered, although he decided, perhaps wrongly, to ignore the fact that his embassy was being treated as a tribute mission (1). In general he found much to admire in China. He had an audience with the Emperor at the summer residence at Jehol. He failed to perform the kotow (the ritual of three prostrations and nine head-knockings required at an imperial audience) but he was nevertheless given a dignified reception and he recorded this fully in his journal (2). A less favourable view was expressed by John Barrow, a member of his suite (3). Dr Gillan, the embassy's physician, was consulted by the Grand Secretary, the emperor's notorious favourite Ho-shen, and he recorded his views on Chinese medicine, asserting the value of western methods of diagnosis over the Chinese doctrine of the pulse and reliance on acupuncture (4).

Macartney's embassy achieved none of the objectives for which it had been despatched and European maritime trade remained confined to Canton. However, the embassy's records provided the starting point for future assessments of China (5). In 1816 another embassy was sent, headed by Lord Amherst. He also refused to kotow and was not granted an audience with the emperor. The failure of the mission may explain the disillusioned view of China expressed by Henry Ellis, Third Commissioner of the embassy (6).

In the early nineteenth century, among those who wrote on China, there was no greater authority than John Francis Davis. Davis, who had accompanied Lord Amherst, learnt Chinese and published translations of Chinese poetry and drama. In *The Chinese*, he attempted to produce the first methodical compilation on China since du Halde's *Description* of one hundred years previously. The tone of the book was favourable towards the Chinese: notably more favourable than that of *China: Before the War and Since the Peace* published *after* the Opium War (7).

Although the frustrations of the Canton trade contributed to the coming of the Opium War, the pre-treaty days of the 1820s and 1830s were recalled as the golden age for westerners in China, at least by the American merchant, W.C. Hunter. Whereas most European merchants conducted their business in pidgin English, Hunter had studied Chinese at the Anglo-Chinese College in Malacca and then worked for Russell and Co. in Canton from 1829–42. In a book published forty years later, he described the life of the *fan kwae* (foreign devils) in Canton. He recorded the security provided for foreigners by the Chinese government and recounted anecdotes of the Hong merchants who had the dubious privilege of holding the monopoly of foreign trade on the Chinese side. He told in particular of the generosity of

Houqua (Wu Ping-chien), the wealthiest of the Hong merchants (8). The British doctor C. Toogood Downing also gave a favourable view of those times. He hoped to introduce his 'good-natured reader' to 'as intimate an acquaintance with this singular people, as the very limited nature of our intercourse will now admit'. But his description of the installation of the Hoppo, the imperial official who was the super-intendent of maritime customs, illustrated the attitude held by west-erners towards the Chinese authorities on the rare occasions that they met (9).

1) *Macartney's view of his reception at the hands of officials*
(Lord Macartney, *An Embassy to China*, pp. 87–8)
The most refined politeness and sly good breeding appeared in the behaviour of all those mandarins with whom we had any connection; but although we found an immediate acquiescence in words with everything we seemed to propose, yet, in fact, some ingenious pretence or plausible objection was usually invented to disappoint us. Thus when we desired to make little excursions from our boats into the towns, or into the country, to visit any object that struck us as we went along, our wishes were seldom gratified. The refusal, or evasion was, however, attended with so much profession, artifice, and compliment that we grew soon reconciled and even amused with it.

We have indeed been very narrowly watched, and all our customs, habits and proceedings, even of the most trivial nature, observed with an inquisitiveness and jealousy which surpassed all that we had read of in the history of China. But we endeavoured always to put the best face upon everything, and to preserve a perfect serenity of countenance upon all occasions.

I therefore shut my eyes upon the flags of our yachts, which were inscribed 'The English Ambassador bringing tribute to the Emperor of China', and have made no complaint of it, reserving myself to notice it if a proper opportunity occurs.

2) *Macartney's audience with the Emperor*
(Lord Macartney, *An Embassy to China*, pp. 122–4)
He was seated in an open palanquin, carried by sixteen bearers, attended by numbers of officers bearing flags, standards, and umbrellas, and as he passed we paid him our compliments by kneeling

on one knee, whilst all the Chinese made their usual prostrations. As soon as he had ascended his throne I came to the entrance of the tent, and, holding in both my hands a large gold box enriched with diamonds in which was enclosed the King's letter, I walked deliberately up, and ascending the side-steps of the throne, delivered it into the Emperor's own hands, who, having received it, passed it to the Minister, by whom it was placed on the cushion. He then gave me as the first present from him to His Majesty the *ju-eu-jou* ... as the symbol of peace and prosperity, and expressed his hopes that my Sovereign and he should always live in good correspondence and amity. It is a whitish, agate-looking stone about a foot and a half long, curiously carved, and highly prized by the Chinese, but to me it does not appear in itself to be of any great value.

The Emperor then presented me with a *ju-eu-jou* of a greenish-coloured stone of the same emblematic character; at the same time he very graciously received from me a pair of beautiful enamelled watches set with diamonds, which I had prepared in consequence of the information given me.... We then descended from the steps of the throne, and sat down upon cushions at one of the tables on the Emperor's left hand; and at other tables, according to their different ranks, the chief Tartar Princes and the Mandarins of the Court at the same time took their places, all dressed in the proper robes of their respective ranks. These tables were then uncovered and exhibited a sumptuous banquet. The Emperor sent us several dishes from his own table, together with some liquors, which the Chinese call wine, not, however, expressed from the grape, but distilled or extracted from rice, herbs, and honey. In about half an hour he sent for Sir George Staunton and me to come to him, and gave to each of us, with his own hands, a cup of warm wine, which we immediately drank in his presence, and found it very pleasant and comfortable, the morning being cold and raw.

Amongst other things, he asked me the age of my King, and being informed of it, said he hoped he might live as many years as himself, which are eighty-three. His manner is dignified, but affable, and condescending, and his reception of us has been very gracious and satisfactory. He is a very fine old gentleman, still healthy and vigorous, not having the appearance of a man of more than sixty. [...]

Thus, then, have I seen 'King Solomon in all his glory'. I use this expression, as the scene recalled perfectly to my memory a puppet show of that name which I recollect to have seen in my childhood, and which made so strong an impression on my mind that I then thought it a true representation of the highest pitch of human greatness and felicity.

3) *Refined civility and gross indelicacy*
(J. Barrow, *Travels in China*, p. 187)
The general character, however, of the nation is a strange compound of pride and meanness, of affected gravity and real frivolousness, of refined civility and gross indelicacy. With an appearance of great simplicity and openness in conversation, they practise a degree of art and cunning against which an European is but ill prepared.

4) *Chinese physicians and the treatment of Ho-shen*
(Lord Macartney, *An Embassy to China*, pp. 280–3)
According to their ideas, every viscus and every part of the body has a particular pulse belonging to itself, which indicates with certainty what part of the system suffers, and how it is affected in disease. They pretend that the pulse, like a general interpreter of animal life, explains every state and condition of the body and that by means of it alone they can immediately discover the seat, nature and cause of disease without asking any question of the patient.... The Grand Secretary, for several years past had been frequently indisposed at various times, and always complained of violent pains ... which generally attacked him about the beginning of spring and at the end of autumn. These pains affected chiefly the larger joints of his arms and legs, his back and his loins. ... It often happened too that he felt excruciating pain about the lower part of the abdomen ... [...]

All these circumstances I learned from himself, and he seemed a good deal surprised at my asking him so many particular questions, which it is not customary for physicians in China to do in any case.... After a full examination of his pulses his physicians had early decided that the whole of his complaints ... were owing to a malignant vapour or spirit ... the method of cure was to expel the vapour or spirit immediately, and this was to be effected by opening passages for its escape directly through the part affected. This operation had been frequently performed and many deep punctures made with gold and silver needles ... [...]

... upon full investigation it appeared that he laboured under two distinct complaints. The first was rheumatism ... [the second] a complete formed hernia.

5) *Reflections on the presentation of the Chinese*
(Review of *Ta Tsing Leu Lee* by Sir George Thomas Staunton, *Edinburgh Review*, 16, 1810, pp. 476–7)
The Chinese have not hitherto had very fair play in Europe. The first missionaries, from the natural propensity of all discoverers to magnify the importance of their discovery, gave a most exaggerated account of their merits and attainments; and then came a set of philosophers, who, from *their* natural love of paradox, and laudable zeal to depreciate that part of their species with which they were best acquainted, eagerly took up and improved upon the legends of the holy fathers, till they had not only exalted those remote Asiatics above all European competition, but had transformed them into a sort of biped Houyhnms – the creatures of pure reason and enlightened beneficence. This extravagance, of course, provoked an opposite extravagance; and De Pauw and others, not contented with denying the virtues and sciences of the Chinese, called equally in question their numbers, their antiquity, and their manual dexterity; and represented them as among the most contemptible and debased of the barbarians, to whom all but Europe seemed to have been allotted in perpetuity. More moderate and rational opinions at length succeeded; and, when our embassy entered the country in 1793, the intelligent men who composed it were as little inclined, we believe, to extol the Chinese, from childish admiration, or out of witty malice, as to detract from their real merits, because they appeared under an outlandish aspect, or had been overpraised by some of their predecessors. The effect of this aspect, however, and this overpraise, were still visible, we think, in the different opinions of the candid and intelligent persons to whom we have alluded. The noble Lord who was at the head of the mission, appears, on the whole, to have formed a higher estimate of this singular people than any of the persons in his train. His ingenious and enlightened secretary, Sir George Staunton, seems to have wavered a good deal as to the point of the scale at which he should place them; and Mr Barrow, though infinitely more accurate and candid than De Pauw, is evidently actuated by something of the same pique or antipathy to the formal orientals, which has given so singular a

colouring to most of the statements and observations of that zealous philosopher.

6) *Recapitulatory remarks on China and its inhabitants*
(H. Ellis, *Journal of the Proceedings of the Late Embassy to China*, p. 440)
I have now exhausted my recollections respecting China and its inhabitants; and have only to ask myself, whether, omitting considerations of official employment, my anticipations have been borne out by what I have experienced? The question is readily answered in the affirmative: curiosity was soon satiated and destroyed by the moral, political, and even local uniformity; for whether plains or mountains, the scene in China retains the same aspect for such an extent, that the eye is perhaps as much wearied with the continuance of sublimity as of levelness. Were it not therefore for the trifling gratification arising from being one of the few Europeans who have visited the interior of China, I should consider the time that has elapsed as wholly without return. I have neither experienced the refinement and comforts of civilized life, nor the wild interest of most semi-barbarous countries, but have found my own mind and spirit influenced by the surrounding atmosphere of dulness and constraint.

7) *On the appearance of the Chinese*
(J.F. Davis, *The Chinese*, I, pp. 253–4)
People in Europe have been strangely misled, in their notions of Chinese physiognomy and appearance, by the figures represented on those specimens of manufacture which proceed from Canton, and which are commonly in a style of broad caricature. A Chinese at Peking might as well form an idea of us from some of the performances of Cruikshank. The consequence has been, that a character of silly levity and farce has been associated, in the minds of many persons, with the most steady, considerate, and matter-of-fact people in the world, who in grave matters of business are often a match for the best of Europeans. Their features have perhaps less of the harsh angularity of the Tartar countenance in the south than at Peking. Among those who are not exposed to the climate, the complexion is fully as fair as that of Spaniards and Portuguese; but the sun has a powerful effect on their skins, and that upper portion of a man's person habitually exposed in the summer is often so different from the remainder, that,

when stripped, he looks like the lower half of a European joined on to the upper moiety of an Asiatic. Up to the age of twenty they are often very good-looking, but soon after that period the prominent cheek-bones generally give a harshness to the features, as the roundness of youth wears off. With the progress of age the old men become in most cases extremely ugly, and the old women can only be described by Juvenal:-

> *'Tales adspice rugas*
> *Quales, umbriferos ubi pandit Tabraca saltus,*
> *In vetulâ scalpit jam mater simia buccâ.'*

> 'Such wrinkles see,
> As in an Indian forest's solitude,
> Some old ape scrubs amid her numerous brood.'

8)*The Hong merchant Houqua*
(W.C. Hunter, *The 'Fan Kwae'*, pp. 49–50)

As another illustration of his generous nature, I may refer to an affair which took place nearly fifty years ago, in which his orders were not complied with. We had shipped a cargo, principally of raw silk belonging to himself, which he had ordered from the silk country. It was sold at a large profit. His instructions were that the proceeds should be returned in East India Co. bills on Calcutta. To our surprise and his disappointment, the result of the sale was invested in a cargo of British goods. It was as injudicious an arrangement (free trade then beginning) to ship largely of English manufactures as his own shipment was sagacious, for but little silk was exported immediately after the opening of the trade. The result showed a difference of many thousand dollars to his detriment. On the deviation of orders becoming known Houqua was at once informed that he should not suffer for this breach of instructions, and for the loss we would credit his account.

The old gentlemen replied, 'My consider, my show you to-mollo' – that is to say, he would think it over and let us know his decision 'to-morrow'. The following day he was at the office, and this was his decision, which he emphasized by striking the floor with his cane – Write to Mr. C—— and tell him he must be more careful in future, 'must take care'. He accepted the woollens, and refused to accept any indemnity.

9)*The installation of the Hoppo*
(C. Toogood Downing, *The Fan-qui in Canton*, III, pp. 80–6)
I happened to be in Canton on the day when the new Hoppo was installed into his office, and had thus an opportunity of seeing the great man when he came into the suburbs. On this occasion, and on no other ... does he show himself to the foreigners. ... The cause of his honouring the Fan-quis with this visit, was doubtless in order that he might know something of the people over whom he was going to exercise his authority. Upon my asking a native, however, for the reason, he told me that the Hoppo would shortly have an audience of the emperor, when his majesty would probably ask him what kind of people the Fan-quis were, and he should look very foolish, if he were to answer that he had not seen them ...

The Hoppo sat in his state carriage, borne along by many coolies, accompanied by the Hong merchants in their sedans, and preceded by the usual number of officers to clear the way. They were received in the state rooms of the British Factory, and after the preliminary ceremonies had been performed on both sides, the Hoppo was invited by the Fan-quis to partake of a breakfast which had been provided for the occasion ...

Along the centre of the spacious apartment a table was placed, spread with a snow-white cloth, and covered with dishes of the greatest delicacies in season. Blancmanges, jellies, and fruits, were abundantly supplied, in addition to the more substantial viands; and, in fact, every thing necessary to form a first-rate breakfast after the English fashion.

On a handsome chair ... sat the Hoppo, surrounded by his numerous attendants respectfully attending to his wishes. He was an old man of about sixty years of age, and of rather a prepossessing countenance. A few gray hairs were growing from the upper lip, and a small tuft of beard was depending from his chin. Attached to the handsome mandarin cap which he wore, a portion of the tail feather of a peacock was to be seen. ... This honorary badge had been given him by his sovereign as a mark of personal favour, and together with the ruby globe which surmounted the cap, indicated the high rank which he filled in the state ...

In order that the Hoppo might have a good view of the Fan-quis, and vice versâ, a slight bannister was fastened up at a little distance on one side of the table. Behind this barrier all the foreigners stood, facing the Chinaman, and watching every movement of his good-natured countenance.

The old man eyed the good things upon the table, and, as he had the whole of them to himself, no one presuming to take a seat, he whispered to his attendants to fetch them for him. As each dish was brought successively, and held up to his eye, he examined it very carefully all around as an object of great curiosity, and then languishingly shook his head, as a sign for it to be taken away. Thus he proceeded for a considerable time, until he had looked at everything on the table, without finding a single article suitable to his delicate stomach.

The foreigners all this while were looking on with very different feelings. Their appetites were wonderfully sharpened by viewing so many good things, especially as it was now the usual time for luncheon. Many of them were witty in their abuse of the old gentleman for his want of taste; and some called him an old fool, and were sorry that they were so situated that they could not show him *how to eat*. However, the Hoppo understood none of these sayings, but quietly proceeded with his examination of the exotic dainties, and when the table had been entirely ransacked, he shook his head once more in sign of disapproval, and then called for a *cup of tea*. The Fan-quis could not bear this; but the greater number left the room, leaving the prejudiced old Tartar to drink his national beverage by himself.

GOVERNMENT AND LAW

The Jesuit description of China in the eighteenth century had emphasized the good government of the country. It also recognized that China had codified its laws before such a practice had been adopted generally in Europe, and that elaborate legal institutions had been developed there.

Respect for these features of China barely continued into the nineteenth century. Frustration with the failure to establish contact with Chinese officials at the appropriate level contributed to the coming of the Opium War, and after China's defeat, many aspects of her system of government received scornful comment from westerners.

Western writings contain many descriptions of leading officials. Sir John Davis, the Governor of Hong Kong, gave a favourable assessment of the senior Manchu official Keying (Ch'i-ying), chief negotiator of the treaty of Nanking and the official subsequently responsible for the conciliatory policy (1). On the other hand, Yeh Ming-ch'en, the Chinese official held responsible for the anti-foreignism encountered in Canton, was portrayed with a combination of fascination and loathing by *The Times'* correspondent, G. Wingrove Cooke, who accompanied him on board H.M.S. *Inflexible* to exile in Calcutta (2). Dr D.F. Rennie described Prince Kung (I-hsin), the leading figure in China's foreign diplomacy at the time of the installation of the British and French legations in Peking in 1861 (3). George Nathaniel Curzon, later to be Viceroy of India, met Li Hung-chang in 1892 and left a record of his impressions of the Chinese statesman (4).

One of the principal objectives of the western powers in China at the beginning of the century was the establishment of diplomatic relations. But when this was finally achieved, by coercion, a strong impression remained that the Chinese could not be trusted in diplomacy. When Canton was captured in 1858, quantities of official documents fell into

British hands and their contents seemed to prove Chinese duplicity at the time of the Opium War. Another flagrant example (from the western point of view) of the Chinese disregard of the canons of acceptable behaviour came in 1860, when Harry Parkes, the man often taken as the epitome of imperialistic attitudes in China, was held prisoner when proceeding to Peking under a flag of truce. This incident prompted the decision to burn the Summer Palace (5).

Other comments about Chinese government are of a more general nature. T.T. Meadows summarized its defects, but added that the system had 'certain peculiar beauties' (6). Another British consular official, W. H. Medhurst, assessed the role of the mandarin (7). The contrast between government in the west and in China, on the level of official intervention, was pointed out by Archibald Colquhoun (8).

An aspect of Chinese government which had long impressed westerners was the use of examinations to select officials. Several westerners, including Archdeacon Gray, himself a Cambridge graduate, were curious enough to visit the Great Examination Hall in Canton and to record the conditions under which examinations were taken there (9). In an article which appeared in 1870, Dr W.A.P. Martin, an American missionary and first President of the Interpreters College in Peking, maintained that the United States might learn from the Chinese on the matter of competitive examinations (10).

Westerners were impressed by the fact that the Chinese had codified their laws. A translation of the Ch'ing penal code was published in 1810 and elicited a favourable comment in the *Edinburgh Review* (11). Nearly a century later, the rationality of Chinese codified law could still be compared favourably with that of ancient Rome (12). But they were appalled by Chinese practices regarding liability and punishment. Dislike of the doctrine of collective responsibility dated back to the *Lady Hughes* case of 1784. A gunner on board a British ship fired a salute which accidentally killed two Chinese. He was surrendered to the Chinese authorities who had him strangled. After that date, westerners refused to hand over accused persons to the Chinese authorities. On 16 June 1844, a Cantonese crowd attacked a group of Americans and in the fracas a Chinese named Hsü A-man was killed. The American Commissioner, Caleb Cushing, refused to allow the matter to be settled in Chinese courts, and in his letter to the United States consul in Canton, he laid down the principles of extraterritoriality, to be incorporated into the treaty of 1844 (13).

Although westerners were no longer answerable to Chinese courts, they remained fascinated with Chinese punishments. Many attended trials and executions and left descriptions of them. Dr H.M. Field, a doctor of divinity, watched the process of judicial torture (14). The interpreter Thomas Taylor Meadows, witnessed the execution of thirty-four rebels at Canton on 29 July 1851 – of these thirty-three were decapitated, but the leader suffered death by slicing (15).

In *A Description of the Empire of China*, du Halde wrote: 'These Prisons are neither so dreadful nor loathsome as the Prisons of *Europe*, and besides are much more convenient and spacious.'[1] A century later the same aspect of the Chinese judicial system excited disgust and the description of the conditions in the prisons of Canton, filed by *The Times'* correspondent George Wingrove Cooke, served to justify the capture and retention of that city during the Anglo-French war (16).

1) *The Manchu official Keying*
(Sir J. Davis, *China*, II, pp. 112–13)
Keying was by far the most elevated in rank, as well as the most estimable in character, of any persons with whom the representatives of European states in China have ever come in contact. During a course of four years' intercourse and negociation, I had a fair opportunity of forming an estimate, and when he only *occasionally* betrayed that departure from conventional stipulations which is the *constant* failing of most Chinese ministers, these instances might be attributed rather to the difficulties of his position than to the bias of his natural temper. This difference between Tartars and Chinese was more than once displayed during the war; it has not escaped the penetration of M. Huc, in the late history of his intercourse with both nations; and Europeans would probably be no gainers in the event of the Tartars being expelled from the empire.

2) *Yeh Ming-ch'en*
(G.W. Cooke, *China*, pp. 397–8)
In his personal appearance Yeh is a very stout and rather tall man, about five feet eleven, with the long thin Chinese moustache and beard, a remarkably receding forehead, a skull in which what the phrenologists call 'veneration' is much developed; a certain degree of

rotundity behind the ear, and a moderate development of the back head. Shorn nearly to the crown, and very thinly covered with hair in that part where the Chinese mostly cultivate their hair, our mandarin offers every facility for craniological examination. His tail is very paltry, very short, and very thin. The smallest porker in China has a better tail than her highest mandarin.

His face is heavy: there is more chin than you usually see in a Chinaman – more jowl and jaw, indicative of will and obstinacy. The nose is long and flat, the nostrils forming one side of a very obtuse angle. Seen in profile, the nose is very remarkable and very ugly; in the front face this, the most simial expression of the man's countenance, is mitigated. The eye – that slit Mongolian eye – is the most expressive feature of the man who is sitting opposite to me, and looking rather suspiciously at me as I am now writing. In his ordinary mood there is only a look of shrewdness and quick cunning in this, the only mobile feature of his face; but I have seen him in the turning moments of his life, when those eyelids opened wide, and those eyeballs glared with terror and with fury. He has a large protruding mouth, thick lips, and very black teeth; for, as he remarks, 'it never has been the custom of his family to use a toothbrush'. It is, however, a very common custom in some Chinese families. . .

3) *The Prince of Kung*
(D.F. Rennie, *Peking and the Pekingese*, I, pp. 42–3)
The Prince of Kung has a very agreeable expression. His features are of the true Tartar type; the right cheek is slightly blemished by two cicatrices, close together, apparently the marks of two small boils. His face and hands are small, the fingers being delicate and effeminate-looking. On the right thumb he wore a large and broad jade-stone ring, of a white colour, with an upper surface of reddish brown. He is about the middle height, and has a slender figure. His dress consisted of a fur robe of the sea otter skin, over a purple silk dress, trimmed with ermine cuffs. His hat was of the ordinary Tartar kind, the turned-up portion being lined with black velvet. The hat was surmounted by a crimson silk knob, in place of the button and high-class peacock's feather, worn by the nobility, or mandarins, as we call them. The Prince had two chains round his neck, one of amber-coloured beads, the other of large beads of red coral. Each of the chains had an

appendage, with precious stones attached, which hung down his back in the same way as his tail. Black satin boots completed his costume.

4) *The Hon. Lord Curzon meets Li Hung-chang, 1892*
(G.N. Curzon, *Problems of the Far East*, pp. 241–2)
At Tientsin I was honoured by the Viceroy with an interview, to which I look back with the greatest pleasure. . . . Carried in green palanquins to the gate, we there descended and passed through one or more dingy anterior courts, small, squalid, and coarsely painted, to an inner room, where seats had been placed round a long table. The Viceroy entered, a tall and commanding figure, considerably over six feet in height, dressed in a long grey silk robe, with a black silk cape over his shoulders. Taking his seat at the head of the table, the Viceroy, with the aid of a competent interpreter, commenced a discussion, mainly upon contemporary politics, which lasted for over an hour. He continually put the most searching and ingenious questions; being renowned, indeed, for his faculty of 'pumping' others about what he desires to ascertain, without emitting the least corresponding drop of moisture himself. While speaking or listening his small, black, restless eyes follow keenly every movement of the features. A big moustache overhangs and partially conceals his mouth, and a sparse Chinese beard adorns his chin. His hair is quite grey and is turning white. Speaking of England, he wished particularly to know whether the recent change of Government involved a change in foreign policy, or whether Mr. Gladstone might be expected to pursue the same line as Lord Salisbury. Upon this point the nomination of Lord Rosebery as Foreign Secretary enabled me to give the Viceroy consolatory assurances. Discussing the tortuous policy which had been followed in relation to the Chinese vassal State which I had just left, he admitted that Korea had been ill-advised, and even allowed that 'there had been ill-advisers in China also'. The Pamirs and Lhasa were the remaining subjects of our conversation, and the Viceroy produced one of the Royal Geographical Society's small maps of the former region.

5) *Chinese disregard of a flag of truce*
(S. Lane-Poole, *Sir Harry Parkes in China*, pp. 235–8)
We had a good six miles to go, and the whole Chinese army . . . between us and our people; but I relied upon our flag of truce carrying

us through. . . . We rode hard, and had only about half a mile more to go to place us in safety, when we got amongst the masses of the Chinese troops. Boom! boom! went a line of guns in their front, which showed that the action had commenced. We held on our way, but as soon as [we] were discovered, horsemen filed off to the right and left of us, and meeting in front, stopped our way. Riding ahead, I called on their officers to allow me and my flag of truce to pass out, but they refused to do this without the order of their General or some superior officer. As the latter did not appear, I with Loch and one sowar with white flag left the party, and rode to the spot where he was said to be. I then after passing through some [tall millet cane] found myself in the presence of a body of matchlock-men . . . we were surrounded by them, and when I called out for the officer I wanted to see, I was pointed to a fat fellow on horseback some distance off on the other side of a creek, and told to dismount and cross over to him.

I now saw that I must be prepared for foul play, but resistance with only three of us . . . being useless, my only hope . . . rested on my flag; and I dismounted and endeavoured to cross the creek to the said officer. While doing so, a greater man appeared, even Sangkolinsin himself, the Chinese Commander-in-Chief; and as he had sent in flags of truce to us on various occasions, I hoped that he would respect mine. . . . But the illusion was soon dispelled, for as I approached I was seized by his attendants and hurled down before him, because I had not instantly obeyed their order to kneel. . .

The moment the Prince gave me an opportunity of speaking to him, which he did by asking me my name, I at once clearly informed him who I was, and of the whole character of my mission to Tung-chow, adding that I was returning to my Ambassador when I was stopped by his troops. I was proceeding with a remonstrance against the treatment I was receiving, when the Prince interrupted me by saying –

'Why did you not agree yesterday to settle the Audience question?'

'Because I was not empowered to do so,' I replied.

The Prince then continued in a very forbidding tone –

'Listen! You can talk reason: you have gained two victories to our one. Twice you have dared to take the Peiho forts; why does not that content you? And now you presume to give out that you will attack any force that stops your march on Tung-chow. I am now doing that. You say that you do not direct these military movements; but I know your name, and that you instigate all the evils that your people commit. You have also used bold language in the presence of the Prince of I, and it is time that foreigners should be taught respect for Chinese nobles and ministers.'

I endeavoured to explain the mistakes of the Prince; told him distinctly what my functions were; that I had come to Tung-chow by express agreement with the Imperial Commissioners, and solely in the interests of peace; and I again begged him to show the same respect to an English flag of truce that we had always paid to those so repeatedly sent in by the Chinese. The Prince, however, simply laughed at all this. . . . On arriving at the house I was again thrown on my knees before him, and the Prince said –

'Write to your people and tell them to stop the attack.'

'It would be useless for me to do so,' I replied, 'as I cannot control or influence military movements in any way. I will not deceive your Highness by leading you to suppose that anything I might write would have such an effect.'

'I see you continue obstinate,' he said, 'and that you will be of no use to me.'

His suite came round and joined in taunting me, and made remarks which indicated very plainly the treachery they had practised, and their own exultation at finding that our army had fallen (as they thought) into their snare. In a few minutes the three of us were put into a cart with two Frenchmen . . . and sent away to the Prince of I . . .

6) *On the defects of Chinese government*
(T.T. Meadows, *Desultory Notes*, pp. 170–1)
The three defects noticed above, are undoubtedly the most serious in the Chinese polity. Were they remedied, were the mandarins only punished when really criminal, and then more rigorously than at present; were their salaries sufficiently raised, and a comfortable competence assured them in their old age; and were they educated for and employed in the discharge of only *one* class of duties, I firmly believe that the system of government in China, considered as a means of securing the happiness of the people, would, from certain peculiar beauties it possesses, prove itself, without either juries or parliament, not altogether unworthy of a comparison with those existing in England and France, and much superior to those acted on in Austria, and some other Christian states.

7) *The Chinese Mandarin*
(W.H. Medhurst, *The Foreigner in Far Cathay*, pp. 80–1)

The general impression out of China is that a mandarin spends his days in idleness and luxury, whilst he battens upon the booty wrung by himself and followers from the unhappy people over whom he is placed; but this is not altogether a correct view. Although little can be said for the general results of mandarin administration in the way of promoting the best interests of the population, and although the wretched pittances allowed by the government as salaries lead to a vast amount of peculation and rapacity, yet the Chinese officials as a class lead a laborious life, and instances are not wanting of individuals winning the esteem and even devotion of the people. Owing to the peculiar system of administration, duties, which, according to our Western ideas, are best distributed amongst a number of officials and departments, are in China concentrated in one individual, and what with judicial business both civil and criminal, finance, police, transport, commissariat, and a number of other heterogeneous duties, a mandarin of any standing always has his hands perfectly full. Office hours commence with the dawn and often only close with the cessation of demands upon the attention which evening of necessity brings. Nor may an official hope for any relief in the diversion which society affords. A mandarin is not expected to have any friendships or intimacies outside of his *yamen*, and he cannot encourage visitors or loiterers within its precincts without laying himself open to a charge of favoritism or corruption. He may not even go out of his *yamen* openly for exercise or recreation. As a rule his secretaries are all-powerful, and in cases where any venality is practised it is always accomplished by or through these men. A *yamen* is in fact practically closed to the public, save through the good offices of a secretary or some other of the numerous underlings who continually haunt its gates and courts. Consequently a mandarin with the best intentions may, even without his privity, become a curse to his neighbourhood.

8) *Chinese democracy*
(A.R. Colquhoun, *China in Transformation*, p. 296)

The great fact to be noted, as between the Chinese and their Government, is the almost unexampled liberty which the people enjoy, and the infinitesimally small part which Government plays in the scheme of national life. It is the more necessary to emphasise this, that a contrary opinion is not uncommon among those who are unacquainted with the country. The Chinese have perfect freedom of industry and trade, of locomotion, of amusement, and of religion, and whatever may be required for regulation or protection is not supplied by Act of Parliament or by any kind of Government interference, but by voluntary associations; of these the Government takes no cognisance, though it may sometimes come into collision with them – never to the disadvantage of the popular institution.

9) *The Great Examination Hall in Canton*
(J.H. Gray, *Walks in the City of Canton*, pp. 511–12)

On our arrival at the gates of the Kuung-Uuen, or Examination Hall, we were, by an aged porter, readily admitted. The hall in question consists of a large quadrangle, which, in form, resembles a parallelogram. Branching, horizontally, from each of two of its sides, are several long rows, or streets of cells. The cells in question, are, in point of number, not less than eleven thousand six hundred and seventy-three. Each, in point of length, is five feet six inches, while, in regard to width, it is not more than three feet eight inches. In front, they are all open. Each cell is, at the time of the examination, furnished with a bed, which consists, simply, of seven, or eight narrow deal boards. The ends of these boards are supported by grooves, which are formed in the side walls of the cell. In the morning of each day of the examination, the candidate, occupying the cell, removes from the grooves, to which we have just referred, two, or three of the boards, which, during the preceding night, formed a part of his bed, and slides them into upper grooves, which are, also, made in the side walls of his cell, in order that they may form, for him, a table on which, by day, to write essays and poems. The boards, which still remain in the lower grooves, serve, of course, as a bench, for him, on which to sit. At the extreme end of each street of cells, there is, for the convenience of the candidates, a large latrine. These streets of cells are, respectively, named by characters, which are taken from the one thousand character classic. Each cell is, also, numbered.

10) *Competitive examinations in China*
(W.A.P. Martin, *The Chinese*, pp. 39–40)

The reform proposed in the organization of our civil service, which contemplates the introduction of a system of competitive examinations, makes an inquiry into the experience of other nations timely. England, France, and Prussia have each made use of competitive examinations in some branches of their public service. In all these states the result has been uniform – a conviction that such a system . . . affords the best method of ascertaining the qualifications of candidates for government employment. But in these countries the experiment is of recent date and of limited application. We must look farther East if we would see the system working on a scale sufficiently large and through a period sufficiently extended to afford us a full exhibition of its advantages and defects.

It is in China that its merits have been tested in the most satisfactory manner; and if in this instance we should profit by their experience, it would not be the first lesson we have learned from the Chinese, nor the last they are capable of giving us. . . . Nor is it too much to affirm that, if we should adopt the Chinese method of testing the ability of candidates, and of selecting the best men for the service of the State, the change it would effect in our civil administration would be not less beneficial than those that have been brought about by the discoveries in the arts to which I have referred.

The bare suggestion may perhaps provoke a smile; but does any one smile at the idea that we might improve our polity by studying the institutions of Egypt, Rome or Greece?

11) *The Penal Code of China*
(Review of *Ta Tsing Leu Li* by Sir George Thomas Staunton, *Edinburgh Review*, 16, 1810, pp. 481–2)
Our readers, we suppose, would not thank us for an exact account of the divisions, books and sections of this Chinese Code. . . . It will probably suit their purpose better, if we endeavour . . . to point out what struck us as most remarkable in the general character of the work, and then specify such of its enactments as appear to us to throw any valuable light on the genius and condition of the people, or on the nature of their peculiar institutions.

And here, we will confess, that by far the most remarkable thing in this code appeared to us to be its great reasonableness, clearness and consistency – the business-like brevity and directness of the various provisions, and the plainness and moderation of the language in which they are expressed. There is nothing, here, of the monstrous *verbiage* of most other Asiatic productions – none of the superstitious deliration, the miserable incoherence, the tremendous *non sequiturs* and eternal repetitions of those oracular performances; – nothing even of the turgid adulation, the accumulated epithets, and fatiguing self-praise of other Eastern despotisms; – but a calm, concise, and distinct series of enactments, savouring throughout of practical judgment and European good sense, and, if not always conformable to our improved notions of expediency in this country, in general approaching to them more nearly than the codes of most other nations. When we pass, indeed, from the ravings of the Zendavesta, or the Puranas, to the tone of sense and of business of this Chinese collection, we seem to be passing from darkness to light. . . . And, redundant and absurdly minute as these laws are, in many particulars, we scarcely know any European code that is at once so copious and so consistent, or that is nearly so free from intricacy, bigotry and fiction. In every thing related to political freedom or individual independence, it is indeed wofully defective; but, for the repression of disorder, and the gentle coercion of a vast population, it appears to us to be, in general, equally mild and efficacious. The state of society for which it was formed, appears incidentally to be a low and a wretched state of society; but we do not know what wiser means could have been devised for maintaining it in peace and tranquillity.

12) *Chinese and Roman law compared*
(E. Alabaster, *Notes and Commentaries on Chinese Criminal Law*, pp. 614–17)
It will surprise many to learn the number of similarities between the Law of Rome – more especially at its maturity – and that of China. . .

So at the start there is the resemblance in the manner by which the present Chinese Code at its inception and Justinian's Codes were formed respectively . . . – in either case a solicitous Emperor being aided by distinguished scholars. And of other likenesses in this connection: between the discouragement of publications additional to the Chinese Code (save by authority), and such in Rome: between the *Li*, and enactments supplementary to the Justinian Code: between the respective manners of legislating by edicts, decrees, and rescripts.

And next of the stated law.... As regards the law touching relationship in China and the conditions prevailing between parent and child ... husband and wife, master and slaves and freedmen, master and pupil – and again on such general points as adoption, and copartnership of relations in the family estate ...

As regards procedure and administration there are also points akin: of administration, perhaps between the ... sitting magistrate in China, and the *judex* – and the remedies for injustice lying against both functionaries: of procedure, certainly in such points as appeal – in both states the appeal resting ultimately with the Emperor, but commonly with a select Board (the Judiciary Board in China, the *consistorium* in Rome).

Finally there is the general position and condition of the professional class in China at the present day – not very dissimilar to its position in Rome prior to Diocletian.

Such are a few of the analogies between two at first sight very different systems. But the comparison is not intended to be pressed too closely, or possibly two or three very incorrect conclusions will be evolved by the ingenious – for instance, that the Chinese system is behind the times: or possibly even that China has been much indebted to Rome or *vice versâ*. No, the curious points are not these, but this – that two races shut off from each other should have thought and moved much alike. The Chinese system is not behind the times of China – but it is admirably suited to them; nor is the system an ancient curiosity or relic – but the evolved production of 4000 years.

13) *Legal jurisdiction over foreigners in China*
(H.B. Morse, *The International Relations of the Chinese Empire*, I, p. 329)
The nations of Europe and America form a family of States, associated together by community of civilisation and religion, by treaties, and by the law of nations.

By the law of nations, as practised in Europe and America, every foreigner, who may happen to reside or sojourn in any country of Christendom, is subject to the municipal law of that country ...

In the intercourse between Christian States on the one hand, and Mahommedan on the other, a different principle is assumed, namely, the exemption of the Christian foreigner from the jurisdiction of the local authorities ...

One or other of these two principles is to be applied to the citizens of the United States in China. There is no third alternative. Either they are to be surrendered up to the Chinese authorities, when accused of any breach of law, for trial and punishment by the magistrates of China, or (if they are to have protection from their country) they come under the jurisdiction of the appointed American officer in China.

In my opinion, the rule which obtained in favour of Europeans and Americans in the Mahommedan countries of Asia is to be applied to China. Americans are entitled to the protection and subject to the jurisdiction of the officers of their government. The right to be protected by the officers of their country over them, are inseparable facts.

Accordingly, I shall refuse at once all applications for the surrender of the party who killed Hsü A-man; which refusal involves the duty of instituting an examination of the facts by the agency of officers of the United States.

14) *The use of judicial torture*
(H.M. Field, *From Egypt to Japan*, pp. 378–80)
In another case, two men were accused of robbery with violence – a capital offence, but by the Chinese law no man can be punished with death unless he confesses his crime. . . . Of course in a case of life and death he will deny it as long as he can. But if he will not confess, the court proceeds to take stringent measures to *make* him confess, for which purpose these two men were now put to the torture. The mode of torture was this: There were two round pillars in the hall. Each man was on his knees, with his feet chained behind him, so that he could not stir. He was then placed with his back to one of these columns, and small cords were fastened around his thumbs and great toes, and drawn back tightly to the pillar behind. This soon produced intense suffering. Their breasts heaved, the veins on their foreheads stood out like whipcords, and every feature betrayed the most excruciating agony . . .

While these poor wretches were thus writhing in agony, I turned to the judge to see how he bore the spectacle of such suffering. He sat at his table quite unmoved; yet he did not seem like a brutal man, but like a man of education, such as one might see on the bench in England or America. He seemed to look upon it as in the ordinary course of proceedings, and a necessary step in the conviction of a criminal. He used no bravado, and offered no taunt or insult. But the cries of the sufferers did not move him. . . . He sat fanning himself and smoking his pipe, as if he said he could stand it as long as they could . . .

But still the men did not give in, and I looked at them with amazement mingled with horror, to see what human nature could endure. The sight was too painful to witness more than a few moments, and I rushed away. . . . I confess I felt a relief when I went back the next day, to hear that they had not yielded . . .

Horrible as this seems, I have heard good men – men of humanity – argue in favor of torture, at least 'when applied in a mild way'. They affirm that in China there can be no administration of justice without it. In a country where testimony is absolutely worthless – where as many men can be hired to swear falsely for ten cents apiece as you have money to buy – there is no possible way of arriving at the truth but by *extorting* it. No doubt it is a rough process, but it secures the result. As it happened, the English gentleman who accompanied us was a magistrate in India, and he confirmed the statement as to the difficulty, and in many cases the impossibility, of getting at the truth, because of the unfathomable deceit of the natives. Many cases came before him in which he was sure a witness was lying, but he was helpless to prove it, when a little gentle application of the thumbscrew, or even a good whipping, would have brought out the truth . . .

15) *Death by slicing*
(T.T. Meadows, *The Chinese and Their Rebellions*, pp. 655–6)
As soon as the thirty-three were decapitated, the same executioner proceeded, with a single-edged dagger or knife, to cut up the man on the cross: whose sole clothing consisted of his wide trousers, rolled down to his hips and up to his buttocks. He was a strongly-made man, above the middle-size, and apparently about forty years of age. The authorities got him by seizing his parents and wife; when he surrendered, as well to save them from torture as to secure them the seven thousand dollars offered for his apprehension. . . . As the man was at the distance of twenty-five yards, with his side towards us, though we observed the two cuts across the forehead, the cutting off of the left breast, and slicing of the flesh from the front of the thighs, we could not see all the horrible operation. From the first stroke of the knife till

the moment the body was cut down from the cross and decapitated, about four or five minutes elapsed. We should not have been prohibited from going close up, but as may be easily imagined, even a powerful curiosity was an insufficient inducement to jump over a number of dead bodies and literally wade through pools of blood, to place ourselves in the hearing of the groans indicated by the heaving chest and quivering limbs of the poor man. Where we stood, we heard not a single cry; and I may add that of the thirty-three men decapitated, no one struggled or uttered any exclamation as the executioner approached him.

16) *The Canton prisons*
(G.W. Cooke, *China*, p. 372)
A Chinese gaol is a group of small yards enclosed by no general outer wall (except in one instance). Around each yard are dens like the dens in which we confine wild beasts. The bars are not of iron, but of double rows of very thick bamboo, so close together that the interior is too dark to be readily seen into from without. The ordinary prisoners are allowed to remain in the yard during the day. Their ankles are fettered together by heavy rings of iron and a short chain, and they generally also wear similar fetters on their wrists. The low-roofed dens are so easily climbed that when the prisoners are let out into the yard the gaolers must trust to their fetters alone for security. The places all stank like the monkey-house of a menagerie.

We were examining one of the yards of the second prison, and Lord Elgin, who is seldom absent when any work is doing, was one of the spectators. As it was broad daylight the dens were supposed to be empty. Some one thought he heard a low moan in one of them, and advanced to the bars to listen. He recoiled as if a blast from a furnace had rushed out upon him. Never were human senses assailed by a more horrible stream of pestilence. The gaolers were ordered to open that place, and refusing – as a Chinaman always at first refuses – were given over to the rough handling of the soldiers, who were told to make them. No sooner were hands laid upon the gaolers than the stifled moan became a wail, and the wail became a concourse of low weakly-muttered groans. So soon as the double doors could be opened several of us went into the place. The thick stench could only be endured for a moment, but the spectacle was not one to look long at. A corpse lay at the bottom of the den, the breasts, the only fleshy parts, gnawed and eaten away by rats. Around it and upon it was a festering mass of humanity, still alive. The mandarin gaoler, who seemed to wonder what all the excitement was about, was compelled to have the poor creatures drawn forth, and no man who saw that sight will ever forget it. They were skeletons, not men.

NOTE

1. J.-B. du Halde, *A Description of the Empire of China*, 2 vols., London, 1738, 1741, I, p. 310.

RELIGION AND SCIENCE

In the eighteenth century Jesuit missionaries observed that the road to riches, honour and employment in China lay through the study of the Confucian classics. As nothing like that was offered for the study of the speculative sciences they were therefore neglected. Throughout the nineteenth century this contrast was frequently repeated, but the observation gained an additional edge with missionaries challenging Chinese religion and with many westerners adding to the critical view of China's current capacity in the sciences.

Western Protestant missionaries in China were both the best – and the worst – observers of Chinese religion. They were the best because their religious training provided them with the vocabulary in which to discuss religion, and their professional life in China ensured that they encountered manifestations of religion more frequently than other foreigners. They were the worst because they arrived with an unshakeable conviction that the religions of China were the product of the powers of darkness, and that their main task was to challenge and defeat them. Nevertheless, among missionaries, there was a great divergence of view on how Chinese religion should be presented. For the Revd W. Ellis, who contributed an introduction to Gutzlaff's *Journal of Three Voyages*, the religion and mythology of China was a 'dark and cheerless system'(1). As in the eighteenth century, Buddhism was viewed as a form of superstition, which, for Protestant missionaries, made it remarkably similar to Roman Catholicism (2).

After the Treaty of Nanking had been signed, a more complex view of Chinese religion was expressed. The Revd Simpson Culbertson considered Chinese religion to be defective (3). The Catholic missionary M. Evariste Huc went further, declaring that the Chinese had nothing worthy to be called a religion (4). His opinion was contested by T.T. Meadows who said that this view derived from the missionary disappointment over the Chinese failure to embrace

Christianity. The true situation was that the Chinese did have religious feeling if that implied a longing for immortality and an admiration for what is good and great (5). The merchant J.R. Scarth compared these views and then recounted two incidents which to him illustrated the extent to which the Chinese might be said to have a real religion (6).

As the century progressed, western scholars, many of them also Christian missionaries, enlarged western knowledge of Chinese philosophy and religion. The Revd J. Edkins suggested reasons why Chinese religion should be studied (7). His interest led him to visit religious buildings, including Confucian temples. But Edkins did not sympathize with the development of a religion of Confucianism, and he had no time for the doctrine of Confucian infallibility (8). James Legge worked on a new translation of the Chinese classics, first published in 1861, which became a classic itself. Legge's estimate of Confucius fell far short of the admiration expressed by the *philosophes* in the eighteenth century (9). The tendency of some sinologues to try to accommodate Chinese mythology to analogous ideas among 'Vedic, Egyptian, Semitic, Greek, Roman, Teutonic, Celtic, and Scandinavian antiquities' was satirized by the Revd E.J. Eitel (10).

Another missionary who followed the scholarly path was the Revd S. Beal, later vicar of Wark-on-Tyne. Beal was interested in Buddhism and through Edkins' researches became aware that the Buddhist Tripitaka, which could shed great light on early Indian history, might be found in Chinese monasteries. At first Beal attempted to persuade the Chinese government to facilitate its purchase, but when that request was refused, he asked Iwakura Tomomi, the Japanese ambassador to Britain, to find a copy in Japan. The India Office was presented with a seventeenth-century edition of the Tripitaka in more than two thousand volumes. Beal estimated that if the volumes were placed one above the other, the collection would reach a height of one hundred and ten feet. He described the collection as 'the groundwork of our knowledge of the Buddhist religion in China and Japan'. Beal was genuinely interested in Buddhism, but his motivation was to advance Christianity. Nevertheless, he was prepared to allow that Buddhism had served the Chinese people (11).

Although missionaries played an important role in the re-evaluation of Chinese religion, and more generally in developing the appreciation of Chinese culture, the attitude that the Chinese as a race lived in darkness which could only be lightened by salvation persisted. It was revitalized by the China Inland Mission, whose founder, Hudson Taylor, was horrified by the enormity of the task which faced the missionary (12).

In the eighteenth century, Chinese knowledge of materia medica, and use of inoculation and acupuncture had earned respect. A century later, with the rapid increase in European scientific knowledge, China's pre-scientific culture attracted derision. Dr Gillan, the physician attached to the Macartney mission, had observed that 'the state of physic ... is extremely low in China'. Nevertheless, for some westerners, Chinese medical knowledge was still of interest. Dr Downing, writing in the 1820s, declared himself not surprised that amid the chaos and confusion and absurdity with which the rationale of the medical profession in China was encumbered, there should still be found many practical and highly useful remedies. However, he applauded the initiative of the American Dr Peter Parker, the surgeon at the Chinese Hospital in Canton, for introducing western medical techniques (14). As the century wore on, it was assumed that the West had nothing more to learn from Chinese materia medica, as shown in Bretschneider's assessment of the value of the *Pen-ts'ao kang-mu*, the sixteenth-century classic by Li Shih-chen (15).

Western views of other aspects of Chinese science were occasionally complimentary, for example in the comparison of the capacity of the Chinese abacus with the prototype computer (16), but more often dismissive. To compensate for this view, the Revd J. Nevius sought to explain the 'peculiarity of Chinese culture'(16), and the Revd E.J. Eitel made sympathetic references to *feng-shui*, that is Chinese geomancy (17).

1) *China: the wonder and the pity of Christians*
(W. Ellis, 'An Introductory Essay on the Policy, Religion, etc. of China' in C. Gutzlaff, *Journal of Three Voyages*, pp. xx–xxi)
The religion and mythology of the Chinese is a dark and cheerless system, blending, with anomalous incongruity, atheism, and the lowest kinds of polytheism; presenting one of the most affecting spectacles in the universe, of the extent and completeness of the calamity, by which the entrance of sin has been attended to our race, shewing millions of mankind joined in one social compact, passing through a long,

uninterrupted series of ages, untaught of life to come, unsanctified, unsaved; following the delusions of their own vain imaginations, or 'worshipping the creature rather than the Creator', who hath 'not left himself without witness among them, in that he did them good, gave them rain from heaven, and fruitful seasons, filling their hearts with food and gladness'. Their creed presents no proper object of reverence, hope, confidence, and love; affords no balm for the troubles of the mind; no support under the ills of life; no hope for the future: their highest prospect is annihilation, or a change by transmigration to the body of some other being in creation. In the language of Dr. Morrison, China is full of dumb idols, is estranged from the true God, and hates and persecutes the name of Jésus; and well may he exclaim, 'China, the wonder and the pity of Christians!'

2) *The priests of Budha*
('Philosinensis', 'Remarks on Budhism', p. 217)
The priests of Budha are a very despised class, sprung chiefly from the lowest of the people. Their morals are notoriously bad, and pinching poverty has made them servile and cringing. They wander abroad in search of some trifling gift, and often encounter many a harsh refusal. Those temples which are well endowed by their founders, are overcrowded with priests, so that only a few among the higher of them can be rich. Neither learning nor skill are found among them, and with a few individual exceptions, they are a very stupid class. Budha, however, seems to have intimated that stupidity brings the votary nearer to the blissful state of apathy, and therefore a knowledge of his institutions is considered the only requisite to form an accomplished priest.

3) *Chinese religion incoherent and inadequate*
(M. Simpson Culbertson, *Darkness in the Flowery Land*, pp. 123–5)
It is to a certain extent true that all are Confucianists – all Tauists – all Buddhists. The same persons may be seen, now in a Buddhist temple – now in a Tauist. A family mourning for a deceased member may call in the Buddhist priests to-day to pray for the soul of the deceased, and to-morrow the Tauist; or both may be called at the same time to perform the services they think needful for the dead.

The explanation of this fact is to be found, probably, in a felt consciousness of some defect in them all. There is in the minds of the mass of the people such a want of confidence in the truth of the doctrines taught, or in the power of the deities worshiped, by these sects, that they adopt the whole, so that if they fail in one place, they may be more successful in another. They are like drowning men who catch at every straw that comes within reach.

4) *The memorials of feeling long since dead*
(M. Huc, *The Chinese Empire*, II, p. 198)

The religious sentiment has vanished from the national mind; the rival doctrines have lost all authority; and their partisans, grown sceptical and impious, have fallen into the abyss of indifferentism, in which they have given each other the kiss of peace. Religious discussions have entirely ceased; and the whole Chinese nation has proclaimed this famous formula, with which everybody is satisfied, *San-kiao-y-kiao*, that is, 'the three religions are but one'. Thus all the Chinese are at the same time partisans of Confucius, Lao-tze, and Buddha; or rather, they are nothing at all: they reject all faith, all dogma, to live merely by their more or less depraved and corrupted instincts. The literary classes only have retained a certain taste for the classical books and moral precepts of Confucius, which every one explains according to his own fancy, invoking always the '*ly*', or principle of rationalism, which has become the only one generally recognised.

But although they have thus made a *tabula rasa* of their religious creeds, the ancient denominations have remained, and the Chinese still like to make use of them; but they are now only the memorials of feeling long since dead.

5) *The religious feeling of the Chinese*
(T.T. Meadows, *The Chinese and Their Rebellions*, p. 66)

M. Huc asserts that the Chinese are destitute of religious feelings. If by this he means nothing more than that the Chinese show no ready aptitude to embrace his form of Christianity, no alacrity to desert the Confucian tablet or the Buddhist idol for the images of the Saints and the Virgin, I fully and thoroughly agree with him. And if Protestant writers mean, when they 'endorse' such opinions, that the Chinese display little intellectual or moral promptitude to adopt their several creeds, which less enforce the great truths of Christianity, as 'peace on earth and good will towards men' than they plant repulsively before the unprepared mind of the heathen the bare results of some centuries of doctrinal disputes, and sectarian bickerings, then, with them likewise I am fully agreed. In that case we are quite at one as to the religiosity of the Chinese. But if by 'want of religious feeling' they mean to assert that the Chinese have no longing for immortality; no cordial admiration of what is good and great; no unswerving and unshrinking devotion to those who have been good and great; no craving, no yearning of the soul, to reverence something High and Holy, then I differ from them entirely and emphatically contradict their assertion. The religious feeling, so understood, is as natural to man as hearing and sight; and I never yet heard of a nation or even a small tribe composed wholly of people deaf and blind. M. Huc himself dilates on the circumstance that China is covered with temples and monasteries, well or richly endowed; and in spite of his after statement that they are the result of an 'old habit', I certainly adhere to the simple and obvious explanation that they are called into existence by strong religious feeling, however ill directed. I may, indeed, here observe that when M. Huc and the other writers, after a positive, sweeping assertion of their psychologically impossible propositions, come to deal with the more palpable facts, they unavoidably contradict themselves. They are then found declaring that throughout the long course of Chinese history, good and great men have abounded, and that heroic spirits have ever come forward to fight and die for what they held to be truth and justice.

6) *Do the Chinese have a real religion?*
(J.R. Scarth, *Twelve Years in China*, pp. 81–2)
It is difficult to define the religion of the Taouists; it is largely connected with astronomy.

One of their chief divinities is Yuh-Hwang Shang-te, the God of Heaven. During a very severe flood at Shanghai, when the waters were at their height, a Taou-sze came down to the banks of the river close to our house; he made a small offering, then knelt down, prayed most earnestly, and, with his face turned to the rushing waters, bowed to the ground in the most abject supplication. The tide never passed the ashes of his offering, and, doubtless, he thought that his prayers for the stay of a public calamity had been kindly answered.

This was the only act of apparently real religion that I ever saw performed by an unconverted Chinese. The purest act of unmitigated idolatry that ever came under my notice was at a short distance from Canton. An old woman knelt on the ground half wailing, half praying, before a paltry paper figure not eighteen inches high. This figure she had placed at the side of the path, at some distance from any house; in front of it burned three wretched little candles, the position of which she changed from time to time – for luck: not content with this, however, she left the extraordinary shrine at which she had been worshipping, and tried her fortune by tossing up some copper coins, watching the manner in which they fell upon the ground, and again reverted to her genuflexions before her paper god.

7) The careful study of the religion of the Chinese
(J. Edkins, *The Religious Condition of the Chinese*, pp. 6–7)

Two results will be observed to follow from a careful study of the religion of the Chinese. The real life of the nation will be better understood, and questions connected with natural theology will receive some fresh illustrations. It will be shown, by new examples, how men, who have not the light of Christianity, seek for something better than they possess, and how they try to satisfy themselves with a substitute, extremely unsatisfactory though it may be, for those truths which revelation teaches.

8) A Confucian Temple
(J. Edkins, *The Religious Condition of the Chinese*, pp. 28–30)

The temples are very numerous, belonging as they do to three religions. They are of all sizes and descriptions. One of those best worth examining is that of Confucius; it is placed in a large area ornamented with trees and water; it includes the government examination-hall, the temple containing the tablets to the national sages, and that in which the distinguished persons of the city are commemorated on monumental boards.

The hall of sages contains the tablets of seventy-two persons ranged on each side of Confucius. . . . He is called, 'the most holy ancient sage Koong-foo-tsze'. By the Jesuits this word was Latinized into Confucius. On the entrance-gates there are inscriptions such as 'The teacher and example for ten thousand generations', and 'Equal with heaven and earth'.

Sacrifices to Confucius are offered at the vernal and autumnal equinoxes. Oxen and sheep are slain, and the carcasses, denuded of the skin, are placed upon stands in front of his tablet. The mandarins are present on the occasion at three o'clock in the morning. The flesh of the ox and the other animals is afterwards divided among the resident literati who may desire it, and eaten by them. The character of the temple is funereal. After entering the gates the visitor passes through a long avenue of cypresses to the chief hall, and the tablets and the mode of placing them are the same as in the funereal temples raised to deceased ancestors. No image is placed to Confucius, except very rarely, and when it is used it is merely as a statue for ornament, not as an idol for worship. The tablet, however, is worshipped. It is called 'the place of the soul'. When Confucius is worshipped, prayers are not made use of; the worshipper is mute while he prostrates himself to express his reverential respect for the virtues of the sage. Those who have rank and property in China join with the learned class in professing to despise all religions but that of Confucius. They associate his name with their ancient national polity, their literature, their system of universal morality . . . [and] they regard him as infallible. Yet he himself was distinguished for humility, and would never have dreamed of claiming infallibility; nor would he have wished to be in that high position of dignity to which his followers have raised him.

9) *The simple views of Confucius*
(J. Legge, *The Chinese Classics*, I, p. 108)
I do not charge the contemptuous arrogance of the Chinese government and people upon Confucius; what I deplore, is that he left no principles on record to check the development of such a spirit. His simple views of society and government were in a measure sufficient for the people while they dwelt apart from the rest of mankind. His practical lessons were better than if they had been left, which but for him they probably would have been, to fall a prey to the influences of Tâoism and Buddhism, but they could only subsist while they were left alone. Of the earth earthy, China was sure to go to pieces when it came into collision with a Christianly-civilized power. Its sage had left it no preservative or restorative elements against such a case.

10) *The amateur sinologue*
(E.J. Eitel, 'Amateur Sinology', p. 3)
If any of our readers wish to be let into the secret in order to apply this novel method to the exposition of all the remaining Chinese Classics,

we recommend to them to study the following recipe, which has been discovered, written in cipher, on a slip of paper which our Amateur Sinologue lately happened to drop. Here it is: Take any Chinese classic, the more ancient the better, strip its heroes of all national and personal characteristics, retaining only their names, make a skeleton abstract of the principal events recorded, put the whole into an old Aryan kettle, throw in sun and moon, five of the planets, and twenty-eight constellations, with the twelve signs of the Zodiac, stir the mass well and let it afterwards settle down till it becomes thoroughly solar, then put the whole into a patent Grimm's philological crucible, to be placed over a slow fire, fed with chips from a German workshop, season the compound well with chopped Sanskrit-Chinese roots, consonants, vowels, prefixes and finals, stir it well and carefully skim off those troublesome Chinese aspirated consonants and tones, keep the mass simmering till you can hear 'the Chinese aspirates and non-aspirates change into Aryan surds and sonants', then take it off and dish it up before the North China Branch of the Royal Asiatic Society, or send it to the Editor of the *China Review*.

11) *The effect of Buddhism on the character of the Chinese people*
(S. Beal, *Buddhism in China*, pp. 259–60)
We sum up, therefore, our estimate of the effect of Buddhism, morally and socially, on the character of the Chinese people in these words:-
Whilst it has not answered any great end in raising the religious tone of the masses of people, it has certainly tended to promote a love of morality, and a healthy state of society, by guarding it against vice or profligacy; and it has helped to raise the mind to a love of the beautiful in nature, and assisted in the advancement of art and literature.

Perhaps, if we were to take the Chinese at the point to which they have advanced – at least, those among them who are Buddhists – and instruct them in a higher wisdom from that point, it would be a right way of using the advantages which their Buddhist culture affords. They are not wedded to idolatry; they have a conception of spiritual truth; they profess to love mercy, and worship an ideal of divine or perfect wisdom. It might be possible to put before them the embodiment of that ideal in the Revelation made to the world of the existence of One who is All-merciful and All-wise.

12) *Mournful and impressive facts about China*

(J. Hudson Taylor, Introduction to M.G. Guinness, *The Story of the China Inland Mission*, I, pp. 9–10)

Were the subjects of the Court of Pekin marshalled in single file, allowing one yard between man and man, they would encircle the globe more than seven times at the equator. Were they to march past the spectator at the rate of thirty miles a day, they would move on and on, day after day, week after week, month after month, and more than seventeen years and a quarter would elapse before the last individual could pass by. Of this vast multitude, in the summer of 1890, 37,287 were communicants in connection with the various Protestant missions. What portion of the seventeen years would it require to watch *them* pass in procession? One single day would amply suffice! Less than three days would permit all the attendants on Christian worship in China to go by; while seventeen years would be needed for the long procession of the heathen. Mournful and impressive fact! Such is the proportion of those who are journeying heavenward to those whose dark and Christless lives, if not speedily enlightened, must end in dark and Christless deaths, and after death the judgment. Two hundred and fifty millions! An army whose magnitude no finite mind can grasp. The number is inconceivable; the view is appalling!

13) *Chinese materia medica*

(C. Toogood Downing, *The Fan-qui in China*, II, pp. 144–50)

There are many drugs which are brought to Europe from China, which are considered by the faculty of our part of the world to possess very excellent qualities, but are almost disregarded by the inhabitants of the country to which they are indigenous. Others again which we believe to be inefficient, and only fit to be thrown out upon the dunghill, are highly esteemed in China and are there worth their weight in gold. The same reflection would probably occur to a Chinese doctor, if he were to inspect a druggist's shop in London; he would often wonder what good effect could follow from swallowing such curious, and apparently disgusting, materials as are there kept. It would be a difficult matter to decide between them, when so many doctors disagree.

The greater number of Chinese medicines are derived from the medical kingdom. There is scarcely a plant to be found in the empire, some part or other of which is not used by the physicians; so that if the notion be correct, that nature has provided in every country for the maladies of its inhabitants, these people have an ample store from which to make their choice ... [...]

Many medicines are also derived from the animal and mineral kingdoms. ... Any dirt or rubbish is occasionally made up into pills by the common order of doctors, and administered with the most beneficial effects to those whose imaginations alone are in fault. In this point, the Chinese do not differ so much from the Europeans as might be supposed. A few years ago our own Materia Medica contained articles of the most ridiculous character, but which are now completely neglected by our more enlightened physicians. At the present time, however, in Russia and elsewhere, the most out-of-the-way substances are administered as medicine.

14) *Assessment of the* Pen-ts'ao kang-mu *of Li Shih-chen*
(E. Bretschneider, 'The study and value of Chinese botanical works', pp. 159, 162)
The pharmaceutical part of the Pên-ts'ao and the therapeutics of the Chinese can only interest us as a curiosity, as far at least as their medical views permit us to judge of the state of their culture. Our materia medica can learn nothing more from the Pên-ts'ao. It is undeniable, that the Chinese possess several very good medicaments, especially stomachics, amara &c., but we possess either the same plants, or others of a similar action. What is profitable among the Chinese medicaments, such as Rhubarb, Camphor, Star Anise, and I may also mention the Tea, we have incorporated many years ago into our pharmacopoeas. The celebrated *Ginseng* ... enjoyed in Europe also a great reputation for some time, but it has been long ago rejected as an expensive and needless medicine. [...]

On the whole it can be said of the Pên-ts'ao, that the descriptions of the plants therein are very unsatisfactory. We find statements of the native country, of the form, the colour of the blossoms, the time of blooming &c. These accounts are insufficient, because the Chinese ... have not a botanical terminology, but the blossoms, leaves, fruits &c., are described, in comparing them with ... other plants, which are often unknown to the reader. Besides these mentioned, there are also statements given about the utility of the plants for economical and industrial purposes. The descriptions consist for the most part of successive quotations of authors, whereby the same statements are several times repeated. Finally Li-shi-chên gives also his own opinion and generally it is the most reasonable one of all. A great many are accompanied with woodcuts, but these are so rude, that very seldom can any conclusion be drawn from them.

15) *The Chinese abacus described by a late literary nobleman*
(Sir J.F. Davies, *Chinese Miscellanies*, pp. 2–3)
'I am informed by Mr Dunn, and by others, that the Chinese perform with it all the operations of arithmetic with equal rapidity and accuracy; so that they must, I conceive, have some simple and almost mechanical process like that for addition. The practical utility of the *Suân-pân*, as used by them, exceeds, beyond all comparison, the far-famed calculating machine of Mr. Babbage, and is such that the mode of working ought to be generally known, and the instrument itself should be generally adopted. It would save much time and trouble, and would also have the advantage of verifying calculations which are made in the ordinary mode. It appears to me to be an object of great curiosity and importance. We have adopted so much from the Chinese already that this would be no great addition to the sum of our obligations.'

16) *Peculiarities of Chinese culture*
(J.L. Nevius, *China and the Chinese*, pp. 280–1)
But it may be asked, 'What have the Chinese ever done? What do they know? Have they ever made a contribution to science? Are they not utterly ignorant of all the modern arts and sciences?' It is true that the Chinese know hardly any thing of the *modern* arts and sciences, and that there is no word in their language to designate some of them; but how much did our ancestors know two hundred years ago of chemistry, geology, philosophy, anatomy, and other kindred sciences? What did *we* know fifty years ago of the steam-boat, the rail-road, and the telegraph? And is our comparative want of knowledge a few years ago and that of our ancestors to be taken as evidence of inferiority of race and intellect? Perhaps this test which some are so ready to apply will, if we go back a few hundred years, establish the claims of the Chinese as a superior race. Printing, which is second in importance to none of the arts of civilization, originated with the Chinese . . .

17) *Feng-shui, or Chinese natural science*
(E.J. Eitel, *Feng-shui*, pp. 6–7)
What has so often been admired in the natural philosophy of the Greeks, – that they made nature live; that they saw in every stone, in every tree, a living spirit; that they peopled the sea with naiads, the forest with satyrs, – this poetical, emotional and reverential way of looking at natural objects, is equally so a characteristic of natural science in China.

The whole system of Feng-shui is based on this emotional conception of nature. We may smile at the unscientific, rudimentary character of Chinese physiology; we may point out, that every branch of science in China is but a rudimentary groping after truths with which every school-boy in Europe is familiar; we may conclude, that China as a whole resembles but an over-grown child, on whose intellect has fallen a sudden blight and who grew up since to manhood, to old age, with no more knowledge than that of a precocious baby; and yet I say, looking at this same China, . . . yet I say, would God, that our own men of science had preserved in their observatories, laboratories and lecture-rooms that same child-like reverence for the living powers of nature, that sacred awe and trembling fear of the mysteries of the unseen, that firm belief in the reality of the invisible world and its constant intercommunication with the seen and the temporal, which characterise these Chinese gropings after natural science.

THE MID-NINETEENTH-CENTURY REBELLIONS

In the middle of the nineteenth century China experienced a series of disastrous rebellions which at one time seemed likely to lead to the overthrow of the Manchu dynasty. The most serious of these was the Taiping Rebellion, 1850–64, the leaders of which adopted a form of Christianity and proposed policies which challenged the Confucian tradition.

The authorities made determined efforts to ensure that the only records of the rebellion to survive should be hostile, and this gives western accounts of it a special value. One such account is of particular poignancy. In a letter addressed to the editor of *The Chinese and General Missionary Gleaner*, the Revd Issachar J. Roberts described how, in about 1846, the future leader of the Taiping Rebellion and his cousin had come to his house, and the former had received religious instruction (1). It was the same Revd Roberts who, years later, was invited to join the rebels at Nanking. His disillusionment with what he witnessed there was expressed vividly in a letter to the *North China Herald* (6).

The first encounters between westerners and the Taipings posed the problem of how to present the rebellion. Capt. Fishbourne, the captain of the *Hermes*, recounted an incident which suggested to him that the rebels were 'quite unlike any Chinese we had ever met' (2). A dramatic encounter was described by T.T. Meadows, the interpreter who accompanied Sir George Bonham on the *Hermes*. He had an interview with the Northern and Assistant Princes, and recorded the moment when they discovered that they were co-religionists (3).

In later years, western attitudes towards the rebellion became increasingly dismissive. After negotiating the Treaty of Tientsin, which opened the Yangtze to foreign navigation once the rebellion had been defeated, Lord Elgin sailed up to Nanking. Although the Taipings made overtures for assistance against the Manchus, British interest now required their suppression and Elgin contributed to that objective (4).

Nevertheless, westerners still contacted the rebels, and came back with contrasting views of the movement. The Revd Joseph Edkins visited Nanking in March 1861, and recorded a sympathetic account of a Taiping Sabbath (5). The view of the Revd Roberts, referred to above, may be contrasted with that of A.F. Lindley, who for four years served as a gunnery instructor with the Taipings. He held a commission from Li Hsiu-ch'eng, the Loyal King, and his book, *Ti-ping Tien-kwoh* is filled with admiring references to the Taiping leader, the outstanding military commander of the later stages of the rebellion (7).

Western accounts of the defeat of the Taipings emphasized the role of Lt.-Col. Charles Gordon, later the hero of Khartoum. He commanded the 'Ever-Victorious Army', which supported the force raised by Li Hung-chang, acting governor of Kiangsu ('the Futai') in the recapture of Soochow. The aftermath of the campaign exemplified the difficulty westerners experienced when co-operating with the Chinese. Among those captured at Soochow were several Taiping 'wangs' or kings. Gordon believed that they had been offered an amnesty and he was furious when Li, suspecting that they planned some treachery, had them summarily executed. The event was widely reported in the British press and Li's duplicitous conduct was contrasted with Gordon's honourable behaviour (8).

Finally, western accounts provide evidence of the devastating effects of the rebellions, for example the plight of refugees in 1861 (9), and the destruction caused by the Moslem Rebellion in Shensi province (10).

1) *The future leader of the Taipings receiving religious instruction*
(I.J. Roberts, *Chinese and General Missionary Gleaner*, p. 68)
I must say that the foregoing narrative . . . looks feasible, and I cannot but believe it in the main. Indeed my own knowledge of the facts corroborates a part of the narrative. Some time in 1846, or the year following, two Chinese gentlemen came to my house in Canton professing a desire to be taught the christian religion. One of them

soon returned home, but the other continued with us two months or more, during which time he studied the scriptures and received instruction, and maintained a blameless deportment. That one seems to be this HUNG *Sawchuen* the chief; and the narrator was perhaps the gentleman who came with him, but soon returned home. When the chief first came to us he presented a paper written by himself, giving a minute account of having received the book of which his friend speaks in his narrative; of his being taken sick, during which he professed to see a vision, and gave the details of what he saw, which he said confirmed him in the belief of what he read in the book. And he told some things in the account of his vision which I confess I was then at a loss, and still am, to know whence he got them without a more extensive knowledge of the scriptures. He requested to be baptized, but left for Kwangsi before we were fully satisfied of his fitness; but what had become of him I knew not until now. *Description of the man.* – He is a man of ordinary appearance, about five feet four or five inches high; well built, round faced, regular featured, rather handsome, about middle age, and gentlemanly in his manners.

2) *Fraternizing with the rebels*
(E.G. Fishbourne, *Impressions of China*, p. 141)
Meanwhile the news soon spread amongst the Insurgents that we were brethren, and numbers came immediately to fraternize. They appeared much pleased at our having our hair long in front like themselves, and that we did not wear tails. The men recently joined had badges sewn on before and behind, to shew that they belonged to the Holy Army. One young fellow, frank and merry-hearted, jumped up to take Sir George Bonham's hat off, to look at his hair, and to admire his hat, which was an ordinary round hat, but he was in contrast to us, as we generally had uniform caps; in doing this, he nearly forced his hat over his eyes, however Sir George was as much amused as the lad himself, and took it very good-naturedly. Numbers continued to flock on board, as the question of friendliness was settled; we weighed, to move closer to the city walls, and many of the Insurgents fell into the capstan to assist, and seemed to enjoy it all as great fun; all in a manner quite unlike any Chinese we had ever met. They at once got on the most friendly terms, and remained so the five days we were there.

3) *Conversation with the Northern and Assistant Princes*
(*Papers Respecting the Civil War in China*, p. 27)

... the Northern Prince, then asked if I worshipped 'God the Heavenly Father?' I replied that the English had done so for eight or nine hundred years. On this he exchanged a glance of consultation with his companion (the Assistant Prince), and then ordered seats to be brought. After I and my companion had seated ourselves, a conversation of considerable length ensued between myself and the Northern Prince. . . . The conversation on my part was turned chiefly on the number and relative rank of the Insurgent Chiefs, and on the circumstances under which they would be prepared to meet Sir George Bonham; but I also explained, as authorized, the simple object of his visit, viz., to notify the desire of the British Government to remain perfectly neutral in the struggle between them and the Manchoos . . .

To all this the Northern Prince listened, but made little or no rejoinder; the conversation, in so far as directed by him, consisting mainly of inquiries as to our religious beliefs, and expositions of their own. He stated that as children and worshippers of one God we were all brethren; and after receiving my assurance that such had long been our view also, inquired if I knew the 'Heavenly Rules' . . . I replied that I was most likely acquainted with them, though unable to recognize them under that name, and, after a moment's thought, asked if they were ten in number. He answered eagerly in the affirmative. I then began repeating the substance of the first of the Ten Commandments, but had not proceeded far before he laid his hand on my shoulder in a friendly way, and exclaimed, 'The same as ourselves! the same as ourselves!' while the simply observant expression on the face of his companion disappeared before one of satisfaction as the two exchanged glances.

4) *The rebels receive a lesson*
(L. Oliphant, *Narrative of the Earl of Elgin's Mission*, II, pp. 317–18)

Upon rounding a bold bluff which projected into the river, we came suddenly upon a small town, built in a recess of the hills, and protected by two or three circular stone redoubts, mounting three or four guns each. These we were inspecting through our telescopes, very much in the spirit in which a Newfoundland would investigate a lap-dog, when, to our amazement, a posse of swaggering rebels came trooping down to the water's edge, dressed, as is usual with them, in many-coloured garments, flourishing yellow and crimson flags, and led by a horseman in a crimson coat and loose white trousers, who looked extremely picturesque, caracolling and vapouring in front of his variegated men. He brandished a matchlock in his hand, which he fired defiantly at us, we being about five hundred yards distant at the time; thereupon his followers exploded, in a futile and absurd manner, all their gingalls at us. This they did two or three times, and we slackened speed to watch their humours; but when they all repaired into one of the circular redoubts, and popped off one of their brass guns at us, we considered the joke had gone far enough, and sent a round-shot whistling over their heads. But the flags waved more defiantly than ever; so the Retribution, making splendid practice, dropped a Moorsom right into the centre of the fort, sending the entire construction into the air, and those of its occupants who were still alive, skimming along the bare hill-side, – their panic-stricken leader, now on foot, rolling repeatedly over and over in his headlong flight, and the bright garments of his soldiers streaming in the wind as they ran after him. The sight tickled Jack's fancy so much that he could scarcely stand by his gun for laughing.

5) *A Taiping Sabbath*
(J.R. Edkins, *Chinese Scenes and People*, pp. 275–7)

The next morning was Saturday (March 23), the rebel Sabbath. We heard that the young chief before mentioned . . . was to preach on the parade ground. Proceeding there we found a large concourse of Taipings. A sea of flags and streamers, red, yellow, white, and green, floated in the wind over them. There was also an assemblage of horses and sedan-chairs. The preacher of the day, who is also in temporary charge of the affairs of the city, and whom we had visited on our arrival, came in a large yellow chair. Beneath the open sky there was a platform made of square tables, and a table on these covered with a red and yellow cloth. On this the preacher stood with his pasteboard yellow coronet, and addressed the listening crowd for twenty minutes. He spoke on the soldier's daily duties, his care of his family, attention to prayer in the night at the appointed time, and observance of the watchword when on guard.

The orator spoke with a weak voice and hesitating manner. He was followed by a more fluent speaker, a high chief, middle-aged, who discussed various moral and political matters. He gave reasons for the exclusion of traders from the city, except such as dealt in medicines, and mentioned locations in which trade may be carried on without the walls. He also referred to the practice of women riding to market; the elder women might do so, but it was not becoming for such as were still young. They had better not be seen in public. He also urged the cultivation of a kind spirit towards the aged and destitute, of whom there were many, and he urged that their case demanded sympathy and aid.

After these addresses, all the listeners . . . knelt towards the table where the young chief also knelt. There was silence for a few minutes, as if they were all praying to the Heavenly Father. Then they rose and separated, feeling perhaps that when a political and moral exhortation had been delivered, and a silent prayer offered to the Heavenly Father, the object of the assembly was gained . . . [. . .]

In the afternoon, when we accompanied Mr. Roberts to preach in a crowded street, a large number of persons stood to listen, and perfect order was maintained while they were addressed upon the truths of Holy Scripture. Mr. Roberts addressed the Taipings who came from the south in the Canton dialect, and I followed him, speaking to the remainder in the Mandarin idiom.

6) *Denunciation of the Taipings*
(I.J. Roberts, *North China Herald*, 8 February 1862)
From having been the religious teacher of Hung Sow-chuen in 1847, and hoping that *good* – religious, commercial and political – would result to the nation from his elevation, I have hitherto been a friend to his revolutionary movement. . . . But after living among them fifteen months, and closely observing their proceedings – political, commercial and religious – I have turned over entirely a new leaf, and am *now* as much opposed to them, for good reasons I think, as I ever was in favor of them. Not that I have aught personally against Hung Sow-chuen; *he* has been exceedingly kind to *me*. But I believe him to be a *crazy man*, entirely unfit, to rule without any organized government; nor is he, with his cooly kings, capable of organizing a government, of equal benefit to the people, of even the old imperial

government. He is violent in his temper, and lets his wrath fall heavily upon his people, making a man or woman 'an offender for *a word*', and ordering such instantly to be murdered without 'judge or jury'. He is opposed to commerce, having had more than a dozen of his own people murdered since I have been here, for no other crime than trading in the city, and has promptly repelled every foreign effort to establish *lawful* commerce here among them. . . . His religious *toleration*, and multiplicity of chapels, turn out to be a farce. . . . It only amounts to a machinery for the promotion and spread of *his own political religion*, making himself equal with Jesus Christ, who, with God the Father, himself and his own son, constitute one Lord over All! Nor is any missionary, who will not believe in his divine appointment to this high equality, and promulgate his political religion accordingly, safe among these rebels. . . . He told me soon after I arrived that if I did not believe in *him*, I would *perish*, like the Jews did for not believing in the Saviour. But little did I then think, that I should ever come so near to it . . . as I did the other day.

Kan Wang, moved by his cooly elder brother . . . and the devil, without the fear of God before his eyes, did, on Monday the 13th inst., come into the house in which I was living, then and there most wilfully, maliciously, and with malice aforethought, *murder* one of my servants with a large sword in his own hand in my presence, without a moment's warning or any just cause. And after having slain my poor harmless, helpless boy, he jumped on his head most fiend-like, and stamped it with his foot; notwithstanding I besought him most intreatingly from the commencement of his murderous attack to spare my poor boy's life.

And not only so, but he insulted *me* myself in every possible way he could think of, to provoke me to do or say some thing which would give him an apology . . . to kill me, as well as my dear boy, whom I loved like a son. He stormed at me, seized the bench on which I sat with the violence of a madman, threw the dregs of a cup of tea in my face, seized hold of me personally and shook me violently; struck me on my right cheek with his open hand; then, according to the instruction of my king for whom I am ambassador, I turned the other, and he struck me quite a sounder blow on my left cheek with his right hand, making my ear ring again; and then perceiving that he could not provoke me to offend him in word or deed, he seemed to get more outrageous, and stormed at me like a dog, to be gone out of his presence. 'If they will do these things in a green tree, what will they do in the dry?' – to a favourite of Teen Wang's, who can trust himself among them . . . ? I then despaired of missionary success among them or any *good* coming out of the movement . . . and determined to leave them, which I did on Monday, January 20th, 1862.

7) *The Chung-wang's levee*
(A.F. Lindley, *Ti-ping Tien-kwoh*, pp. 243–6)
The chiefs all attended the Chung-wang's levee in their state robes and coronets. The Chung-wang himself appeared with a beautiful crown; he was the only chief besides his Majesty, the Tien-wang, who wore one of real gold. The metal was beaten out thin, into beautiful filigree-work and leaves, and formed into the figure of a tiger, the eyes being of large rubies, and the teeth rows of pearls. At each side was an eagle with outstretched wings, and on the top a phoenix. The whole crown was magnificently decorated with large jewels set into the gold, while pearls, sapphires, and other gems hung all around. In his hand the Chung-wang carried a jade-stone sceptre or 'yu-i', curved at each end, and covered with groups of sapphires, pearls, garnets, and amethysts. His state robe was a gorgeous affair, reaching almost to the feet, of beautifully embroidered yellow satin, stiff with gold bosses and dragons worked in gold, silver, and scarlet threads. Yellow embroidered trousers, and boots of yellow satin, similarly ornamented, completed a costume, than which – set off by his handsome and energetic features – it would be impossible to imagine one more magnificent . . .
[. . .]
    The Chung-wang, previous to commencing his march to Ngan-whui, reviewed his body-guard in the large parade ground. This brigade, 5,000 strong, marching under the Chung-wang's standard of green, was composed of one of the finest bodies of men I have ever seen in my life. Until the repulse from Shanghae it was their boast that they had never retreated or turned their backs upon a foe. They were all natives of Kwang-si, the Chung-wang's province, and came principally from the Maoutze, or aboriginal mountaineers . . .

8) *The Murder of the Taiping Wangs*
(A. Wilson, *The 'Ever-Victorious Army'*, pp. 201–2)

This youth was the first to tell Gordon of the execution of the Wangs, on which the Colonel immediately crossed a creek and found on the other side eight of their headless bodies, together with the head of the Na Wang. The bodies were gashed in a frightful way, having been cut down the middle.

On witnessing this sight Colonel Gordon's grief and indignation knew no bounds. Though he had not actually guaranteed the safety of the Rebel Chiefs, yet he had assisted in inducing them to surrender, on the supposition that the Futai would treat them in an honourable and humane manner. His first impulse, when his two steamers came in sight, was to obtain hold of the Futai and inflict summary justice on that high official. General Ching, however, gave timely warning of Gordon's incensed state, and Li very wisely hurried into the city, thus avoiding a meeting. For some days after this Gordon's anxiety to meet with the Futai was only equalled by that of the Futai to keep out of his way, and this was the only period of his campaign during which the Commander of the Ever-Victorious Army burdened himself with carrying arms. When he reached the Futai's boat, which he did very soon, he found it empty, and had to content himself with leaving a letter upbraiding Li for his treachery. After this Colonel Gordon departed in his steamer for Quinsan, taking with him the Na Wang's son and the head of that unfortunate Chief. He had ordered up his force to assist him in seizing the Futai, but [he] . . . brought them back to their quarters . . . and read to them with great agitation an account of what had happened at Soochow, concluding with the statement that, as a British officer, he could not serve under the Futai any more unless the Peking Government should take steps to punish such treachery.

9) *Refugees*
(T.W. Blakiston, *Five Months on the Yang-tsze*, pp. 260–1)
Before leaving Sü-chow, however, I must not omit to say that, on a visit to the pagoda . . . opposite to the city at the mouth of the Min, we found a great number of refugees, – poor country people who had deserted their homes and fled before the advance of the rebels. They were mostly from the districts up the Min; and though a panic is sufficient to drive people from their homes, the small amount of anything in the shape of baggage which these unfortunates had about them attested a very rapid retreat. A great many were taking shelter in

the buildings of the temple just below the pagoda, men, women, and children, some of the last still at their mothers' breasts; young girls of delicate form and appearance, as if used to polite society, and looking as if the tattered clothes they then wore ill befitted them; also there were old grey-bearded men and infirm old women, who must have had their physical powers well tested to have been able to reach this place of refuge. But amidst this scene the young men were playing at cards; and so infatuated are the Chinese in this practice of gambling, that I believe any number would be found willing to sit around a barrel of gunpowder with a slow match attached, if they knew that, for the period of time which must elapse before the match would ignite the powder, they could not play anywhere else, although the moment after they would be hurled into eternity.

10) *Effects of the Moslem Rebellion in Shensi*
(A. Williamson, *Journeys in North China*, I, pp. 369–70)
Hoa-chow, once populous and flourishing, now presented a most melancholy aspect. There was literally not one house standing entire; many were level with the ground, and all were unroofed. The only habitable places were two or three houses temporarily covered with thatch, and occupied by men from the yamun. We lodged outside the west gate . . . in a miserable inn which was in process of rebuilding. We could get nothing to eat but bean-cake curd; and no dishes to eat even that in, but broken and dirty crockery. The rebels first had carried off almost everything, and the patriotic soldiers had made a clean sweep of the little that was left. There was not a pig nor a fowl to be seen, save one cock, which we asked the man to cook for us; but he politely requested us to excuse him, as he kept this cock to awaken the guests and carters in the morning . . .
October 16th. – Next day the ruins of towns and cities were yet more numerous; almost every turn of the road revealed fresh atrocities. As we passed along, village after village was lying in the dust, the only things standing upright being the iron poles which stood before the temples. In the afternoon we saw a most painful sight, as we ascended a hill and skirted round it; for we came in view of a fine plain, in which were some ten or twelve villages, with only the walls in some places standing. We were told that for about 100 miles, at one time, there was not a living man to be found.

SOCIAL LIFE

Under the Treaty of Nanking, 1842, and subsequent treaties (known collectively as the 'unequal treaties'), China had been forced to open selected ports to the west for trade and residence, to surrender control of external tariffs and to release westerners from liability to Chinese law. For most westerners life in China meant life in the treaty ports, the ports opened under the unequal treaties. Western writings contain many descriptions of the Chinese as seen in those communities. Two examples are cited: Canton described by George Wingrove Cooke, *The Times'* special correspondent (1), and Hankow, opened to foreign trade and residence in 1861 as seen by a British medical missionary John Kenneth Mackenzie (2).

Western accounts of China often described the social classes. References to the gentry were nearly always hostile (3). For many westerners, the closest contact they had with Chinese was as an employer or in a master/servant relationship. Robert Hart, a trainee interpreter and future head of the Chinese Imperial Maritime Customs, was familiar with both relationships (4). Edward Bowra, a clerk in the same service at Tientsin, starting on a salary of £400 per annum in 1863, could afford an entourage of six servants (5). Although labour was so cheap, there was also slavery in China (6).

Of the classes in Chinese society, perhaps the one most frequently referred to was that of beggars. Mendicancy was no novelty to Europeans, but its prevalence in the treaty ports, and its organization made it noteworthy, as was also the provision, or otherwise, of relief for the poor (7 and 8).

When describing habits and customs, some writers were struck by contrasts between western and Chinese life; others emphasized points of comparison, for example in matters of fashion (9), and on the social significance of opium-smoking (10). Travellers often refer to the hygienic practices of the countries which they visit. Western comments on Chinese practice varied greatly: Macartney's experience at the Manchu court left him extremely critical (11), but sixty years later, when the contrast between European and Chinese standards of hygiene might be expected to have widened, Elgin held a contrary view (12).

Western accounts record features of Chinese life which were found amusing or repulsive because they contrasted with the experience of the traveller in his home country. Two examples are included: the Abbé Huc's account of the 'cat clock' (13), and a passage from the Revd Justus Doolittle's *Social Life of the Chinese* – perhaps the richest source of this type of comment (14).

1) *The pure and uncontaminated city of Canton*
(G. Wingrove Cooke, *China*, pp. 75–6)
People who have never seen an unadulterated Eastern city are apt to entertain very erroneous ideas upon the subject. When we are told of a city of a million of inhabitants we begin to think of the Rue Rivoli, or of Regent Street, or of the Corso, or of the French buildings and Moorish palaces at Algiers, or, at least, of the great squares of Alexandria, or the European quarter at Cairo. We must put European houses entirely out of the question when we think of the pure and uncontaminated city of Canton. With the exception of the pagodas, the josshouses, and the yamuns, there is not in the whole city an edifice as high as the lowest house in Holywell-street. The mass of habitations are about fifteen feet high, and contain three rooms; they have one entrance, closed by a bamboo screen. Some of the shops have a low upper story, and then the house, roof and terrace altogether, may rise twenty-five feet from the street. Better houses there are, but they are not more lofty. They are detached, stand upon their own little plot of land, and are surrounded by a twelve-foot wall. Then there are the palaces, residences of great officials and rich merchants, the 'yamuns' of governors, and generals, and judges. These are large airy buildings, situated in gardens extensive enough to be called parks – excellent barracks and camping-ground for British grenadiers.

All these edifices are of the most fragile description, built of soft brick, wood, or mud; no hopeful shelter to the most desperate courage. They would be traversed by Minié balls and pierced by grape; they would be knocked into ruins by half-spent round shot; they would be burst by shells ...

2) *Hankow in the 1870s*
(Mrs Bryson, *John Kenneth Mackenzie*, pp. 44–5)

'It is indeed surprising to see a Chinese city,' he [Mr Mackenzie] writes; 'the streets are so narrow that no such thing as a carriage or cart could possibly get through. In some of the medium-sized streets I could almost touch both sides by stretching out my arms, and in the widest of the Hankow streets not more than four or five people could stand abreast. Yet these narrow streets are alive with people all day long; all heavy goods are carried through on wheelbarrows, or on coolies' shoulders. By the aid of a bamboo pole one coolie will carry a tremendous weight, balancing it on his shoulder with the weights suspended at each end of the pole. They carry buckets of water from the river in this fashion. The richer people are carried in sedan chairs, and every one has to make way for them. You will therefore believe me when I say that locomotion through a Chinese street is a somewhat difficult matter. The shops have no windows, but expose their wares directly to the public gaze. For protection from thieves every shop-owner keeps a dog. The Chinese dogs are mostly the size of a large retriever; they are extremely ugly and savage, but very cowardly. One cannot go about without a stick, for they always recognise a foreigner, and set up a savage howl; if you have a stick in your hands, however, they take care to keep at a respectable distance; without this they will attack you. To-day I saw a man professing to extract worms from another man's teeth to cure toothache.'

3) *A hostile view of the gentry*
(C. Toogood Downing, *The Fan-qui in China*, I, pp. 238–9)

It may be an itinerant tinker . . . who impedes your progress: and it may be the next instant the gay, light boat, which carries a gentleman to pay his morning visits – there he sits in state, under a small square canopy, supported only at the corners with thin round poles; his dress made of fine white linen, blue silk and damask, with his fan in his hand and his tea on a small table by his side. This appearance would bespeak a Chinese gentleman, even if you did not observe the whiteness of his hands and the extreme delicacy and sickliness of his countenance, very different from the brown ruddy hue of health of the lower orders.

In fact the Chinese gentry, as far as I have seen, with some few exceptions, have a sickly, unprepossessing look. There is more than mere effeminacy to be observed in the faces of the upper classes of the Celestial citizens; there is something which excites in many strangers a disgust and antipathy to them, even at the first glance.

4) *Consular employees at Ningpo*
(Robert Hart, *Journals*, p. 138)
The Writer Shin heang ting drowned his brother some days ago. This young man was behaving so very badly that it was feared he wd commit some action which might disgrace or ruin the family. Accordingly, the father being dead, & the management of the concerns of the family having devolved upon Shin the eldest son, after some deliberation he fixed on this mode of getting rid of his brother. So he put his head in a sack & assisted by another brother he took him to the jetty & held his head under the water till he was dead. No one could guess from his appearance that anything unusual had happened. However I understand that people outside rather dislike to associate with him now; & Mr. Meadows with whom he writes Chinese seems desirous of sending him about his business.

Engkwei, the Head servant, though married ten or more years has had no children. And as ten years, the usual period assigned to patient expectation, have elapsed without produce he bought a little boy about two years old to be his son. The price was 5000 cash about 15/-[15 shillings]. A grand feast was given by Engkwei to his friends the other evening; in the middle of the entertainment the little fellow was brought out & presented to the guests, all of whom rose & bowed to him. I noticed that the Consular servants *sat* at one table; while the guests, who were not connected with the Consulate, had a table to themselves. The little chap comes into me sometimes & seems greatly delighted with the pictures.

5) *The entourage of a clerk in the Imperial Maritime Customs*
(C. Drage, *Servants of the Dragon Throne*, pp. 67-8)
They are six in number, not one of whom can speak a word of English. First comes my *Sien Sheng* or teacher, a grey, pig-tailed, old gentleman of most respectable appearance and reverend mien. I have given him a room to live in and I pay him 20 dollars or about £5. Next comes my 'Boy' or body servant, of about 25 years of age and with a fair share of intelligence, who performs all the multifarious duties of valet, house-maid and boots; sews the buttons on my shirts, mends the rents in my

clothes and is always at my elbow when I want him. He receives the sum of $5 monthly or about £1 sterling. A couple of coolies to sweep the yard, fill and empty my bath, carry me to my sedan chair or perform any duty I like to command, together with my *marfoo* and my horse, complete the number and fill up the list.

Finding that riding was the only exercise practicable here and that horses were marvellously cheap, I invested in a fine, cream coloured animal with good quarters and promising speed, for which I gave 40 dollars or £8. As *Marfoo* or groom, I engaged a sharp sort of fellow calling himself 'Ah Chu' at the rate of $5 a month and $5 more for the horse's fodder. Thus for £2 a month I have a luxury which at home would cost me £100 a year.

Cooks etc. are joint property and included in the mess account which, with wine, beer and everything, does not come to more than £18 or £20 a month. For this you live in capital style, two or three kinds of wine, joints, poultry, game fish, vegetables and fruit such as Covent Garden could scarcely rival. This is truly a marvellously cheap country.

6) *Slavery in China*
(J.H. Gray, *China*, I, pp. 241–2)
In the families of Chinese gentlemen, female servants generally, and male servants in some instances, are the property of their masters by purchase. In the houses of wealthy citizens, it is not unusual to find from twenty to thirty slaves attending upon a family. . . . The average price [of a slave] is from fifty to one hundred dollars, but in time of war, or revolution, poor parents, on the verge of starvation, offer their sons and daughters for sale at remarkably low prices. I remember instances of parents, rendered destitute by the marauding bands who infested the two southern *Kwangs* in 1854–55, offering to sell their daughters in Canton for five dollars apiece. . . . Amongst the many Chinese friends and acquaintances I made during my residence at Canton, one, an old man named Lum Chi-kee, was what may be termed a slave-broker; and I remember two bright-looking youths being sold to him by their profligate father, who had gambled his means away. . . . The old slave-broker offered one of the youths to me at the advanced price of 350 dollars. . . . Before buying slaves, a dealer keeps them for a month on trial. Should he discover that they talk in their sleep, or afford any indications of a weakness of system, he either

offers a small sum for them, or declines to complete the purchase. . . .
A slave is carefully examined by an intending purchaser especially as to
any signs of leprosy. . . . The broker is made to take the slave into a
dark room, and a blue light is burned. Should the face of the slave
assume a greenish hue in this light, a favourable opinion is entertained.
Should it show a reddish colour it is concluded that the blood is tainted
by this loathsome disease.

7) *Beggars in Foochow*
(J. Doolittle, *Social Life of the Chinese*, II, pp. 262–3)
When burials connected with wealthy families take place on the hills,
or the regular annual sacrifices to the dead are about to be performed
in the spring at their graves, beggars often interfere for the purpose of
getting food or money. . . . Oftentimes a considerable sum of money is
distributed on such occasions among the beggars before they will allow
the burial or the sacrifice to proceed. . . . According to the superstitious views of the Chinese, the burial should take place at a time fixed
by the fortune-tellers in order to be propitious, and the beggars take
advantage of this fact to hinder and harass, in the hope of getting more
money to keep quiet. On the occasion of the burial of a native
Christian at this place in 1857, a company of beggars and of lepers
gathered around the grave, and demanded twenty thousand cash as the
condition of allowing the coffin to be lowered into the grave. One of
the rabble actually got down into the grave, and thus prevented the
lowering of the coffin. The burial was delayed . . . until near dark,
when, finding, contrary to usual custom, that no hour was fixed for the
consummation of the burial, and that their exorbitant demands would
not be complied with, they were glad to accept eight hundred cash, to
be divided among themselves, and the coffin was lowered to its
position and the burial completed.

8) *The poor-law in Canton*
(Lt.-Col. Fisher, *Personal Narrative of Three Years' Service in China*,
pp. 37–8)
A great many beggars die in Canton: I do not mean to assert a mere
truism, but actually die out in the open air: a good many in the public
streets; but there is a court-yard in the western suburb which appeared
set apart for this express purpose . . .

With the poor-law, which we were told exists in Canton, I wonder how any one can ever die simply of starvation. Any man may go about with a couple of bits of bamboo, and enter a shop, and bang his bamboos together until he is given money to go out; but for the smallest coin (the tenth part of a halfpenny), he is bound to go away, and is free to inflict his music elsewhere. Now what can be better? The poor-rate is voluntary, nay, even self-imposed; no one is forced to contribute to support these vagrants, and yet all do. No one who has strength to crawl from house to house, and clatter his bamboos, need ever starve; at the same time the smallness of the coin given is not sufficient to make it worth while for idle persons to trust solely to such a subsistence, if other means can be got. So think of it, oh ye boards of guardians, and imagine parishes where the relieving officer is not known, poor-rates are a relic of barbarous ages, and the householders voluntarily keep the whole of the destitute, and no one is on the parish!

9) *Chinese dress*
(T.T. Meadows, *Desultory Notes*, p. 9)
The Chinese dress – to descend to minor topics – is generally supposed to be quite unchangeable, and the Chinese tailors a kind of stereotype clothiers. Now it is true that the Chinese (I speak of the middle and higher classes) always wear long gowns when they go out, just as we wear coats; but as every part of our coats and our other garments are constantly subjected to all kinds of changes, within certain limits, so the length of the Chinese gown, the size and form of its sleeves, its colour, and the kind of flowers worked in it when of silk, &c. &c. are perpetually varying. The same is the case with the Chinese shoes and winter scull-caps: the former are, within certain limits, at one period thick and at another thin-soled; and the latter are at one time shallow and at another deep, while the silk knob on the top is sometimes small, at others large, &c. &c. In China, in short, we find as many fops as in Europe, who, like their brethren of the West, are so thoroughly versed in matters of dress, that they can at a glance tell you whether a man's clothes be of the latest fashion or not.

10) *Opium-smoking compared with alcohol abuse*
(W.A.P. Martin, *A Cycle of Cathay*, pp. 85–6)
At Ningpo I began to study the effects of opium-smoking. . . . The conclusion to which I was brought is, that to the Chinese the practice is an

unmitigated curse. Whether it is worse than the abuse of alcohol among us I shall not undertake to decide. The contrast between the effects of the two drugs is remarkable. Liquor makes a man noisy and furious; opium makes him quiet and rational. The drinker commits crime when he has too much; the opium-smoker when he has too little. Drinking is a social vice, and drunkenness a public nuisance; opium-smoking is mostly a private vice, indulged at home; but even in opium-shops it is more offensive to the nose than to the eye or ear. Alcohol imprints on the face a fiery glow; opium, an ashy paleness. Alcoholic drinks bloat and fatten; opium emaciates. A drunkard may work well if kept from his cups; an opium-smoker is good for nothing until he has had his pipe. A drunkard can in most cases cure himself by force of will; the opium habit is a disease, which to break from requires, in all cases, the help of medicine. It takes years for alcohol to reduce a man to slavery; opium rivets its fetters in a few weeks or months. It does not take the place of tobacco, which, used by all classes as a more or less innocent indulgence, is indispensable to the opium-smoker; nor does it take the place of alcoholic drinks, which are consumed as much as ever. Even its moderate use unfits a man for most pursuits. . . . In the long run, the insidious drug saps the strength, stupefies the mind, and of course shortens the span of life. Its expense, though great in the aggregate, is nothing in comparison with the loss of time and energy sure to follow in its wake.

11) *Hygiene in China*
(Lord Macartney, *An Embassy to China*, p. 225)
They wear but little linen or calico, and what they do wear is extremely coarse and ill washed, soap being never employed by them. They seldom have recourse to pocket handkerchiefs, but spit about the rooms without mercy, blow their noses in their fingers, and wipe them with their sleeves, or upon anything near them. This practice is universal, and what is still more abominable, I one day observed a Tartar of distinction call his servant to hunt in his neck for a louse that was troublesome to him . . . [. . .]

They have no water-closets nor proper places of retirement; the necessaries are quite public and open, and the ordure is continually removing from them, which occasions a stench in almost every place one approaches.

12) *Chinese bathing establishments*
(*Letters of James Earl of Elgin*, p. 92)
I forgot to mention that I visited the town of Shanghae yesterday, and among other things went into a bathing establishment, where coolies were getting steamed rather than bathed at rather less than a penny a head, which penny includes, moreover, a cup of tea. So that these despised Chinamen have bathing-houses for the million. With us they are a recent invention: they have had them, I believe, for centuries. I am told that they are much used by the labouring class.

13) *The 'Cat-clock'*
(M. Huc, *The Chinese Empire*, II, pp. 315–16)
One day when we went to pay a visit to some families of Chinese Christian peasants, we met, near a farm, a young lad, who was taking a buffalo to graze along our path. We asked him carelessly, as we passed, whether it was yet noon. The child raised his head to look at the sun, but it was hidden behind thick clouds, and he could read no answer there. 'The sky is so cloudy', said he, 'but wait a moment'; and with these words he ran towards the farm, and came back a few minutes afterwards with a cat in his arms. 'Look here', said he; 'it is not noon yet'; and he showed us the cat's eyes, by pushing up the lids with his hands. We looked at the child with surprise, but he was evidently in earnest: and the cat, though astonished, and not much pleased at the experiment made on her eyes, behaved with most exemplary complaisance. 'Very well', said we; 'thank you'; and he then let go the cat. . . .

To say the truth, we had not at all understood the proceeding; but we did not wish to question the little pagan, lest he should find out that we were Europeans by our ignorance. As soon as ever we reached the farm, however, we made haste to ask our Christians whether they could tell the clock by looking into a cat's eyes. They seemed surprised at the question; but . . . we related what had just taken place. That was all that was necessary; our complaisant neophytes immediately gave chase to all the cats in the neighbourhood. They brought us three or four, and explained in what manner they might be made use of for watches. They pointed out that the pupil of their eyes went on constantly growing narrower until twelve o'clock, when they became like a fine line, as thin as a hair, drawn perpendicularly across the eye, and that after twelve the dilatation recommenced.

When we had attentively examined the eyes of all the cats at our disposal, we concluded that it was past noon, as all the eyes perfectly agreed upon the point.

14) *Reverence for lettered paper*
(J. Doolittle, *Social Life of the Chinese*, II, pp. 168–9)
A society, called 'Lettered-paper Society', having from eight or ten to a hundred or more members, exists quite numerously here, the object of which is to secure the Chinese character from irreverent use. Generally, each society erects a furnace in which to burn to ashes the waste paper its agents may collect. Each employs one or more men, whose business is to go around the streets and alleys, collecting every scrap of lettered paper which may have fallen to the ground, or which may be found adhering loosely to the walls of houses or shops. Some men gather together refuse lettered paper, old account-books, advertisements, etc., which they sell to the head man or agent of these societies, often getting only half a cent per pound, or even a less sum . . .

The ashes of this paper are carefully put into earthen vessels and kept until a large quantity is collected. They are then transferred to baskets, and carried in procession . . . to the bank of the river, where they are either poured out into the water, and allowed to float down into the ocean, or placed in a boat and taken several miles down the river. . . . A band of musicians is hired to accompany the procession, who play on their instruments as they pass along the streets. The members of the society carry each a large stick of incense, already lighted, held reverently in one hand before them as they pass along.

WOMEN AND CHILDREN

It is an obvious, but important point to note that westerners, when making particular observations about China, drew upon the experiences and value judgements of their own society. This point is well illustrated by references to the position of women and children in China: the comparison which is being made – whether implicit or explicit – is with their position in Europe and the United States. One of the events most commonly described was the marriage ceremony. William Milne, a Protestant missionary who attended a marriage in Shanghai in 1853, emphasized the contrasts between Chinese practices and those followed in the west (1).

As the century progressed the dominant view among westerners was that Chinese women were debased and degraded (2). A particular issue was the emphasis placed on the chastity of widows. W.H. Medhurst wrote a touching description of the suicide of a woman after her fiancé had died (3). Dr Gray, the Archdeacon of Hong Kong, witnessed the consequences of a wife being suspected of unchastity by her husband (4).

Exceptionally, the Taiping rebels permitted their women to occupy a more emancipated position in society – a situation noted in several western accounts of the rebellion (5).

One aspect of the position of women and children in China which was frequently commented upon was the supposed prevalence of female infanticide. Perhaps attention was paid to this matter because it was also an issue in Victorian England – the opprobrium cast on the Chinese may have drawn attention away from a social problem which still existed in Europe. Views on the prevalence of female infanticide in China differed widely, and the contradictory statements illustrate a problem encountered when using sources of this kind. The Revd Charles Gutzlaff was convinced that female infanticide was practised ruthlessly in Amoy (6); Capt. Fishbourne claimed to have first-hand

---

71

knowledge of the frequency of infanticide (7). The widely travelled Abbé Huc alleged the practice was widespread – Catholic missionaries, who practised infant baptism, were especially concerned about this issue (8). But W.H. Medhurst, the British consul at Shanghai, was not convinced that the practice was so common, and other writers supported his view (9). Infanticide seemed incompatible with the affection which the Chinese displayed towards their children. The care they extended to orphans and abandoned children, as Dr Gordon, Deputy Inspector-General of Hospitals, Army Medical Department, observed, was comparable to that currently available in England (10).

The custom affecting women which received almost universal comment was foot-binding. The Revd William Milne, writing in the 1850s, thought the fashion no more pernicious than others adopted in the west (11). However, Mrs Bryson, of the London Mission, Tientsin, who wrote a popular book about Chinese children, was in no doubt that the custom was pernicious (12). Missionaries played an important role in establishing the Natural Foot Society, which had Mrs Archibald Little as its first President (13).

Many of the descriptions of the condition of women in China were written by missionaries, who were not usually found enjoying the company of a Chinese mistress. But European men often had relations with Chinese women and Robert Hart recorded his thoughts on this subject, though he destroyed the pages of his journal which covered the years of a long-term liaison he enjoyed (14).

Most comments referred to women in China Proper, and applied to women of Chinese descent. Descriptions of the lifestyle of women elsewhere in the Chinese Empire often contrasted their demeanour with that of Chinese women, presenting them as easy-going and accessible (15).

1) *The inspection of the bride*
(W.C. Milne, *Life in China*, pp. 153–4)
I was much surprised to find the bridal chamber open to public gaze and scrutiny. And at this as at other weddings, two or three features forced themselves on me, as exceedingly *outré* to the notions of a Westerner. To any special visitor who entered, the bride was brought out for inspection, and at the interview he was at liberty to offer what remarks he might think *apropos*, about her lips, nose, eyes, eyebrows,

feet, petticoats, &c. Evidently the remarks were stale and commonly current; for, when one experienced hand made his observations, they were responded to by appropriate sentences from another in the crowd. However outrageous all this was to me, a mere looker-on, it was amazing to mark the composure of the young bride through it all; – not a smile on her lips, – not a muscle moved, – not a blush in her face; and I was then informed that the reputation of a bride greatly depended on the gravity, calmness, and temper, with which she received the remarks of bystanders at such a time.

2) *The status of women in China*
(M. Huc, *The Chinese Empire*, I, pp. 248–51)

The condition of the Chinese woman is most pitiable; suffering, privation, contempt, all kinds of misery and degradation, seize on her in the cradle, and accompany her pitilessly to the tomb. Her very birth is commonly regarded as a humiliation and a disgrace to the family. . . . If she be not immediately suffocated . . . she is regarded and treated as a creature radically despicable, and scarcely belonging to the human race . . . [. . .]

This public and private servitude of women – a servitude that opinion, legislation, manners, have sealed with their triple seal – has become, in some measure, the corner-stone of Chinese society. The young girl lives shut up in the house where she was born, occupied exclusively with the cares of housekeeping, treated by every body, and especially by her brothers, as a menial, from whom they have a right to demand the lowest and most painful services. The amusements and pleasures of her age are quite unknown to her; her whole education consists in knowing how to use her needle; she neither learns to read nor to write; there exists for her neither school nor house of education; she is condemned to vegetate in the most complete and absolute ignorance, and no one ever thinks of, or troubles himself about her, till the time arrives when she is to be married. Nay, the idea of her nullity is carried so far, that even in this, the most important and decisive event in the life of a woman, she passes for nothing; the consulting her in any way, or informing her of so much as of the name of her husband, would be considered as most superfluous and absurd.

The young girl is simply an object of traffic, an article of merchandise to be sold to the highest bidder. . . . On the day of the wedding there is great anxiety to adorn and beautify her. She is clad in splendid robes of silk, glittering with gold and jewels; her beautiful plaits of raven hair are ornamented with flowers and precious stones; she is carried away in great pomp, and musicians surround the brilliant palanquin, where she sits in state like a queen on her throne. You think, perhaps, on witnessing all this grandeur and rejoicing, that now, at last, her period of happiness is about to begin. But, alas! a young married woman is but a victim adorned for the sacrifice. She is quitting a home where, however neglected, she was in the society of the relations to whom she had been accustomed from her infancy. She is now thrown, young, feeble, and inexperienced, among total strangers, to suffer privation and contempt, and be altogether at the mercy of her purchaser. In her new family, she is expected to obey every one without exception. . . . She has no right to take her meals with her husband; nay, not even with his male children: her duty is to serve them at table, to stand by in silence, help them to drink, and fill and light their pipes. She must eat alone, after they have done, and in a corner; her food is scanty and coarse, and she would not dare to touch even what is left by her own sons.

3) *Suicide of a Chinese lady*
(W.H. Medhurst, *The Foreigner in Far Cathay*, pp. 104–6)
Apropos of visiting and cards . . . I may here allude to a most singular circumstance connected with a card which I once received in China. It was from a lady, intimating her intention to commit suicide at a specified date. She was very young and attractive, and belonged to a wealthy family. Unfortunately, the Chinese gentleman, to whom she had been affianced from childhood, had died just before the date fixed for their nuptials, and she gave out that she deemed it her duty to render her widowhood irrevocable by dying with her betrothed. So she sent cards round to the neighbouring gentry, giving notice of the purpose I have mentioned. No attempt was made by her relatives or by the local authorities to frustrate the insane design, the general opinion, on the contrary, being that she was about to perform a meritorious act. I even went so far as to appeal to the mandarins to put a stop to the proceeding, but they assured me that interference on their part might lead to a popular demonstration. Eventually, on the day named, the woman did deliberately sacrifice her life in the presence of thousands.

A stage was erected in the open fields, with a tented frame over it, from which was suspended a slip of scarlet crape; one end of this she adjusted round her neck. She then embraced a little boy, probably a little brother, presented by a person standing by, and having let fall a veil over her face, she mounted a chair and resolutely jumped off it, her little clasped hands saluting the assemblage as her fast-failing frame twirled round with the tightening cord.

4) *The price paid for suspicion of unchastity*
(J.H. Gray, *China*, I, pp. 223–4)
The most serious charge, however, upon which a Chinese husband can obtain a divorce from his wife is that of unfaithfulness. Even a suspicion of this exposes her, however innocent she may be, to much harsh treatment at his hands. I remember an instance, which occurred in 1861, of a gentleman named Foong Kām-sām, beating his wife to death on the bare suspicion that she had been unfaithful to him. This monster of cruelty resided in a street of the western suburb of Canton. . . . It appeared from inquiries which I made on the spot, that the poor woman had gone from home for two or three hours during the evening in question, to witness a religious festival. On her return her husband accused her of unfaithfulness, and, binding her hand and foot, deliberately flogged her to death. When I entered the house on the following day, I found the almost naked corpse of the poor woman stretched on the floor. It presented a very sad spectacle, the whole body, more especially the head, face, and shoulders, being very much lacerated. The mother of the murdered lady had stationed herself outside, on the opposite quarter of the street; and, in a state of frenzy, she continued to speak to the passers-by of the brutal conduct of her son-in-law for several hours. The murderer was taken to prison, but not so much, I apprehend, in the character of a prisoner, as of one from whom the authorities were simply anxious to obtain an explanation of the circumstances attendant on the violent death of his wife. I was present at the police court when the wretch was undergoing his examination, and was not a little astonished when his discharge from further confinement was ordered by the magistrate.

5) *Women in Taiping society*
(G.J. Wolseley, *Narrative of the War with China in 1860*, p. 345)

In Nankin, the population of which is now very small, there are about two women for every man. Most of the inhabitants have been captured, a large proportion having been taken from Soochow; and unlike any other town which I had hitherto visited in the empire, the women walked and rode about in public, and did not pretend, as Chinese ladies usually do, to be in the least degree afraid of foreigners, nor did they seek to shun us. They were almost all beautifully dressed in the curiously worked silks and satins of Soochow. With admirable discrimination the followers of the Heavenly King seem exclusively to reserve the good-looking women in the almost general massacres which follow their victories. Old women and female children there were, we may say, none, although there was a very large proportion of boys. To be the husband of one wife does not necessarily form part of the new faith, the spiritual revelation regarding which, has been made to serve even such vile purposes as the suspension, in particular cases, of the tenth commandment.

6) *The drowning of new-born female children*
(Revd C. Gutzlaff, *Journal of Three Voyages*, pp. 174–5)
This constant emigration of the male part of the people contributes very much to the destruction of domestic happiness. It is a general custom among them to drown a large proportion of the new-born female children. This unnatural crime is so common among them, that it is perpetrated without any feeling, and even in a laughing mood; and to ask a man of any distinction whether he has daughters, is a mark of great rudeness. Neither the government nor the moral sayings of their sages have put a stop to this nefarious custom. The father has authority over the lives of his children, and disposes of them according to his pleasure.

7) *Female infanticide common in China*
(Capt. E.G. Fishbourne, *Impressions of China*, p. 14)
Infanticide is by no means the worst, and for this there is a tolerable pretext in the stern necessities under which they live – they are driven to great straits. There are millions always on the verge of starvation, and it is equally certain that thousands annually perish from want; thousands of the female children of the very poor are drowned: the only alternative presenting itself to them is that of selling them to slavery and the lowest degradation.

To my own knowledge this practice of infanticide was continued up to a recent period at Amoy and Shanghae; and the bodies of infants so drowned were to be seen any day in a pond at Amoy, or in a creek adjoining the city at Shanghae, by those who chose to satisfy themselves on the point.

8) *The suffocation and drowning of infants*
(M. Huc, *The Chinese Empire*, II, pp. 347–8)

As for ordinary infanticides – the suffocation and drowning of infants – they are innumerable, more common, unquestionably, than in any other place in the world, and their principal cause is pauperism. From the information we have collected in various provinces, it appears that persons in embarrassed circumstances kill their new-born female children in the most pitiless manner. The birth of a male child in a family is an honour and a blessing; but the birth of a girl is regarded as a calamity especially with necessitous parents. A boy is soon able to work . . . the family is continued also by a boy. . . . A girl, on the contrary, is a mere burden. According to Chinese manners, she must remain shut up till the period of her marriage, and she cannot exercise any kind of industry, by which she might make amends to her parents for the expenses she occasions. It is therefore the girls only that are murdered, as they are regarded as causes of indigence. In certain localities, where the culture of cotton, and the breeding of silkworms furnish young girls with suitable occupations, they are allowed to live, and the parents are even unwilling to see them marry and enter another family. Interest is the supreme motive of the Chinese, even in cases where the heart alone ought to have influence.

9) *A nation of infanticides?*
(W.H. Medhurst, *The Foreigner in Far Cathay*, pp. 89–90)

The Chinese have the credit amongst most Englishmen of being a nation of Infanticides, and the impression is to be attributed to the stories which cursory visitors, and even observing travellers, are apt to bring home. These will tell, it may be, of 'baby towers', standing in the vicinity of most towns, and of suspicious little bundles noticed in pools and canals; of carts which are said to go round for the purpose of collecting castaway children; of miniature coffins strewed about the fields, &c. Such things have no doubt intruded themselves upon the notice, but the observers have not taken the trouble, or, perhaps, from ignorance of the language, have not always found themselves able to inquire, how or why these remains came to be so disposed of. Had they done so, they would have learnt that the relics seen were by no means in every instance, or even nearly so, those of castaway or murdered infants, the Chinese being one of those people who do not consider it essential to give formal sepulture to a child under a certain age. The truth in this, as in most other cases, may be discovered to lie between the two extremes. There are towns and districts where infanticide is practised, in some to an infamous extent, in others to a less degree; there are others again where it is not known at all as a habit, and in the majority of cities I am inclined to believe that it is a crime no more indulged in than is the case in some European towns, and then only with the object of concealing another act of frailty. If there is any distinction to be made, it is in favour of the northern and midland, as against the southern and coast provinces.   But as a rule one has only to enter a Chinese city or hamlet to be convinced that the stories about infanticide must . . . have been exaggerated, for the swarms of children of both sexes which lounge about the doors and infest the gutters is something remarkable. The Chinese, moreover, exhibit a marked attachment to their offspring.

10) *The Foundling Hospital, Tientsin*
(C.A. Gordon, *China from a Medical Point of View*, pp. 140–3)
One of the most interesting public institutions in Tein-tsin that I had an opportunity of visiting was the Foundling Hospital. . . . Above the door is placed a tablet, bearing upon it an inscription in Chinese . . . 'The Hall for Cherishing Children'. Entering under this tablet, we passed along a passage and . . . were met by some of the people connected with the establishment who, recognising the consul, at once offered to conduct us over the entire place. There seemed at the time of our visit to have been about twenty children, together with their nurses, accommodated in each of these enclosures; the total number of foundlings in the establishment being about eighty; and it may be observed that so general in this part of China is the fashion of compressing the feet, that those of the unfortunate female inmates of this establishment were being subjected to this process. There is no separate portion of the building appropriated as an hospital for the

sick; the children are attended by native physicians in their own dormitories or court-yards. One division, however, is appropriated to a class of children and grown people whose melancholy condition is calculated to command the pity of all visitors. Here the inmates were composed of the blind, the deaf, the dumb, and the idiotic of both sexes, together with their attendants; and here we were informed that while, as a general rule, the other children are not retained after they have attained the age of fourteen years, the unhappy creatures for whose use this particular portion is devoted, are retained for life if necessary. . . . Arranged upon tablets on either side of the hall were the code of regulations of the establishment, and lists of the principal benefactors and contributors to its funds; these reminding us of what we were accustomed to see in charitable institutions at home . . . [. . .]

The children brought in are, in some instances, of a class corresponding to that from whom institutions in England, similar to this one, derive their distinctive names. In other instances, infants are brought in by their parents, when the latter are too poor to maintain them, and in such instances are often claimed when the pecuniary circumstances of the father or relations become more propitious.

. . .We were also informed that some of the children in the institution are adopted by people who have no family of their own, and it would appear that comparatively few remain in it until they attain the age of fourteen. Those who do remain so long are then sent away, the boys to learn trades – each receiving a donation of ten taels – the girls, to be married, with a dowry of fifteen taels each, or about £5 sterling. The fact deserves to be stated, however, that the girls are always placed in a respectable position in life, never being abandoned to vice and infamy.

I have entered at some length into a description of this institution, because few people, personally unacquainted with China, would suspect the existence of such a one in that country. It is, moreover, satisfactory to state that, at the time of our visit the children within its walls looked remarkably healthy, although personal cleanliness was evidently a matter altogether beneath the notice of their attendants. There was not among them more than a fractional part of the squalling that there would be among one quarter the number of children in the United Kingdom, and the arrangement of everything connected with the place was quiet and orderly.

11) *The effects of foot-binding*
(W.C. Milne, *Life in China*, pp. 13–14)
It cannot be doubted that cases of gangrene have occurred from such severe compression of the foot; and loss of both feet, or of life, and other evils, might be detailed as arising out of this pernicious rule of fashion. But . . . I incline to the opinion that the injurious effects to life and health from this tortuous position, are not so certain as has been imagined. Mr. Lockhart, in his 'Medical Missionary Report of his Hospital at Chusan, in the year 1840–41', observes: 'Though several females came to the hospital affected with various diseases and with ulcers of the leg, only in one or two instances was there seen any ulcer or other disease apparently caused by the compression of the foot and the forced distortion of its bones. It cannot be said with any degree of certainty how far this practice is injurious to health; but it would appear . . . that it does not cause so much misery as might be expected from the severe treatment to which the feet are subjected in infancy. And torturing as this treatment of the feet would appear to be, and unsightly as are its consequences, it is, perhaps, on the whole, not more injurious to health and comfort than are the practices inflicted by fashion on the female sex in Western nations.'

If there really be pain or distress in feet so tightly bandaged, it is marvellous to watch the evident freedom from both, shown by women who can walk several miles a day, – or by nurses, that seem to bear about their infant charges without discomfort, – or by maid-servants, who with apparent ease perform more than the ordinary amount of duties undertaken by English servants. There is nothing like the distress we should expect shown by the young women, who, with feet like hoofs, go through strange posture-making dances, or by the little girls that play about the streets and lanes. Women are fond of playing at shuttlecock, and, for the battledore, use the cramped foot. . . . I have seen, in a company of travelling jugglers, a woman raise a four-legged table upon her two club feet, balance it in the air, and turn it round and round upon her two extremities, but without manifesting pain.

12) *Foot-binding*
(Mrs Bryson, *Child Life in China*, pp. 96–7)
This deformity is produced, not by iron or wooden shoes, as is sometimes supposed, but by narrow cotton bandages about three yards long. They are applied when the little girl is six years old.

One end of the strip of cotton is placed beneath the instep, and then carried over the four small toes, drawing them down beneath the foot. Another twist draws the heel and great toe nearer together, making an indentation beneath the sole. When all the cloth has been used, the end is firmly sewed down, and the feet are left for a week or two in that condition. Clean bandages are now and then put on, but the change has to be very rapidly effected, or the blood begins again to circulate in the poor benumbed feet, and the agony becomes almost unbearable. Not unfrequently during the process a girl loses one or two of her toes; but she feels repaid for the pain she endures by being the possessor of still smaller feet. Mothers and nurses frequently perform this duty for their daughters, and in passing a Chinese home one sometimes hears the bitter crying of a child whose feet are being bound.

Yet so strong is the power of fashion, that, sooner than be unlike other girls, or have to bear the derision of their neighbours, who will laugh at them and say, 'Just look at those two boats going by', in reference to their large feet, they prefer to endure the pain. I have known cases of little girls, whose parents had been induced by the missionaries to refrain from binding their feet, who would actually procure bandages and try to do the binding themselves.

13) *An anti-foot-binding meeting in Canton*
(Mrs Archibald Little, *The Land of the Blue Gown*, pp. 312–13)
Dr Kerr ... presided on the occasion and told a curious story of the greatest compliment, that had ever been paid to his medical skill, when some twenty years or more before a lady had come from afar to put herself under him as a patient. Both her feet had mortified off through binding; she had however brought them with her – *in spirits*, and now wanted the foreign doctor ... to fasten them on for her again. How many women in China would be thankful if this could be done ... !
The captain of a Chinese man-of-war, who had previously studied at Yale College, most kindly served as an interpreter, and from the eager attention and bursts of laughter it was evident not a point was lost. Though once or twice the gallant captain paused visibly, and looked with some hesitation at the screened-off side of the chapel, where amongst the other women sat his own wife, known as one of the richest as also one of the tightest-bound ladies of Canton. He however gathered up his courage and interpreted bravely, and I have never

addressed an audience, that seemed so much moved as that Cantonese audience, if one might judge by their laughter, generally a pretty fair indication in China, or by the way in which they all crowded up to the top of the chapel to pay each a small sum of money, and receive a paper indicating their association with the Natural Feet Society.

14) *On taking a Chinese mistress*
(Robert Hart, *Journals*, Sunday, 29 October 1854, p. 71)
My salary wd not support an English wife: such a person is considered a great 'bother' out here: delicate – sickly – demanding great attention, medical care, and numerous servants, &c. &c.; such is the condition of an English lady in China. Now some of the China women are very good looking: you can make one your absolute possession for from 50 to 100 dollars and support her at a cost of 2 or 3 dollars per month. Then our lonely state here makes us wish very strongly for Female society: now, considering all these things, is not my state a very trying one – full of temptation – and that too the most enticing kind?

15) *Women in eastern Tibet*
(T.T. Cooper, *Travels of a Pioneer of Commerce*, pp. 216–17)
The women rarely marry, as a first husband, one of their own class, generally preferring to become temporary wives of the Chinese traders and soldiers . . . a position which is regarded as quite honourable, and in which they observe the most scrupulous fidelity. They are laughing, light-hearted creatures, and make the homes of their Chinese masters very comfortable. Among themselves, they are connected by ties of kindred and friendship, which bind them, as it were in a large clan; and any woman who is deserted by her lord and master, readily finds a home, even if she has no near relations. Their social manners and habits, differ altogether from the secluded life and timid shyness of the Chinese women. They go about and pay visits as they choose, conversing freely with their male friends, without incurring suspicion, and their manner is marked by a child-like freedom from restraint, devoid of the least shade of impropriety. I remember an amusing illustration of this: One morning, four Man-tsu ladies paid me a visit, and were ushered into my room, as I was preparing to wash my hands. I was immediately taken possession of, amid merry shrieks of musical laughter; one held Tang Koopah on her lap, while of the others, one

washed my hands, another my face, and the third stood by with a towel; when this performance, which seemed greatly to amuse them, and certainly did not displease me, was concluded, I presented my fair visitors with some oranges; their dexterous fingers quickly removed the peel in an unbroken piece, which they then twisted in their jet black tresses, each in turn performing her coiffure before my looking-glass, this they told me was a sovereign preventive against sickness.

THE ECONOMY

In the eighteenth century Jesuit missionaries described China as a prosperous society. Du Halde recorded: 'It may be said, without Exaggeration, that China is one of the most fruitful, as well as large and beautiful Countries in the World.'[1] But by the beginning of the nineteenth century this impression had been superseded by a much darker view: in place of prosperity was seen stagnation; increasingly the perception was of economic backwardness, lack of progress and of hardship (1). One of the few achievements of Chinese agriculture was the systematic use of 'night-soil' as manure (2).

Comments on the 'condition of the people' by westerners in China should be treated with caution, as few observers could claim an extensive knowledge of the country. Nevertheless, external comment of this kind, if coming from observant and well-informed writers, has a particular value. The missionary Dr W.H. Medhurst travelled the north-east coast of China in 1835, and described conditions in an area not previously visited by Europeans. His impression was of a population living in reasonable comfort (3).

Some of the best informed comment on the Chinese economy referred to sectors of special interest to Europeans, for example the production of tea. Robert Fortune was sent to China by the Court of Directors of the East India Company to obtain varieties of the tea plant and native manufactures. He carried out his task conscientiously, and played a crucial role in the establishment of tea plantations in the Himalayas. His comments indicate that tea production in China had been adapted to suit the European market, albeit at the cost of dangerous adulteration (4).

Another example of expert appraisal concerned the silk industry. The merchant J.R. Scarth first visited the silk districts near Shanghai in 1848. He later toured the area around Ningpo and described the crude technique used for silk throwing (5). A more exotic commodity investigated by westerners was the insect white wax produced in Szechwan, which was used principally in the manufacture of candles (6).

An aspect of China's economy of which westerners came to have special knowledge was emigration. The Revd C. Gutzlaff, who had encountered Chinese migrants in a number of south-east Asian countries, described emigration from the districts around Foochow in the 1830s (7). As disquiet over the trade in emigrants grew, the Earl of Malmesbury, the Foreign Secretary, asked British consular officials in the treaty ports to reply to a questionnaire. In general their replies are a useful source of information, although the example quoted, that of Acting-Consul Backhouse at Amoy, was criticized for its 'deficiencies'(8).

The subject on which western observers were best qualified to comment was foreign trade. The annual commercial reports made by British consuls in the treaty ports contain a mass of easily-accessible information on this aspect of the Chinese economy. The example given is the report made by Acting-Consul G. Jamieson for the port of Chefoo (Chih-fu) in the province of Shantung (9). The rate of increase of foreign imports into China was a disappointment to westerners, who believed that this was caused by the obstruction of trade by internal customs posts (10).

The establishment of the North China Branch of the Royal Asiatic Society in 1857, and of other learned societies, led to a more systematic collection of information about China. In 1888 the Society sent a questionnaire to various persons 'whose work brought them into contact with the agricultural population', asking for information, for their locality, on the size of agricultural holdings, whether they were owner-occupied or leasehold, how the landlord was paid, what was the annual production and the local selling price and what was the average amount of land tax. The published replies came from eleven missionaries, two consuls and a judge; that from the Revd J.F. Johnson, of the American Presbyterian Mission, Hangchow, Chekiang was one of the briefer responses (11).

By the 1860s, westerners were becoming increasingly interested in China's mineral resources (12). Western capital was used to establish new enterprises and western experts visited China and reported on the progress of these ventures and the employment of a Chinese work-force (13). A number of western observers described Chinese adoption of modern technology. Some of their ventures were praised, but more often their obdurate refusal to recognize the value of new technology was a matter of frustrated comment (14).

1) *Ancient customs in agriculture*
('Agriculture in China', p. 122)
Considering the regard paid by the Chinese to all customs and modes of operation which have the sanction of antiquity, and which are found easy in the execution, we cannot expect that the general plan of conducting agricultural pursuits at present will differ very much from what it was in ancient times. The strictness with which filial duties are enjoined upon the young ... also renders the introduction of any improvement extremely difficult. The great articles of consumption, and the manner of raising them are the same now as thousands of years ago; the implements of husbandry the same; and in the eyes of a Chinese, both are perfect. If improvements, manifest and simple, were proposed to a Chinese husbandman, the proposer of them would be immediately referred to ancient custom ... and this would be an end of all controversy. The force of custom on the minds of the Chinese will be a great bar to their improvement, particularly in agriculture. Experience has shown, that a supply of food can be procured, and a numerous population supported, by an adherence to the ancient mode. And if manual labor is always to be used for animal, it may be well doubted whether these objects can be obtained more perfectly than they are at present. To obtain as large a supply of nourishment as possible in the simplest manner and from the smallest space, is the great end of Chinese agriculture. And to effect this, the land is subdivided into such small portions, that the entire energies of the laborer are directed to a spot not many times larger than the tenement he occupies. Here he must live or starve, and we can easily perceive that he would not be much inclined to waste either land or labor in venturesome experiments.

2) *The use of night-soil*
(R.H. Cobbold, *Pictures of the Chinese*, pp. 155–62)
It is a matter difficult to handle without being offensive to squeamish minds. *The Times'* correspondent ... was almost the first who boldly and plainly spoke out, but it is, nevertheless, one of vast social

importance. Those who remember how Father Thames became, in the drought of last summer, fetid with decomposed matter, threatening the lives of thousands compelled to live in its vicinity, and forcing attention upon statesmen of both Houses of Parliament, may be disposed to listen for a few minutes to what I have to say on the main drainage of large Chinese cities. [. . .]

Be it known, then, that in Chinese cities and towns no underground sewers or drains exist. . . . Rows of large earthen jars, each standing about three feet high by three in diameter . . . are sunk by the sides of thronged thoroughfares . . . over these are built wooden sheds, open towards the road: no attempt at concealment by boarding or doors in front being made. To the European this gives the appearance of gross indecency. . . . [T]he scavenger . . . takes away the contents in his large pails. . . . It is thus moved off into the country, and sold to the farmers . . . [. . .]

The manure is used for almost all the *vegetable* crops. The rice lands are flooded in the early spring, and some deposit is thus obtained to enrich and renovate the soil. They are also sown with a clover-layer, which is ploughed into the land. Bullocks and horses are so few in number . . . that long manure is hardly an appreciable fraction of the whole. All the tribe of vegetables and plants which require to be rapidly developed, such as cabbages, beans, cucumbers, melons, Indian corn, millet, and some of the choicer flowers, are treated with this manure in a liquid state. The instrument used for this purpose . . . is simply a small spouted tub, fixed to the end of a pole. The manure is then poured over the plant, and left to find its way to the roots. This process ceases some weeks before the vegetables are cut for the market; a very necessary fact to be known, but one which, even when known, hardly reconciles the foreigner to the sight of Chinese greens on his dinner-table. It is generally allowed that an excessive quantity of manure imparts a strong and disagreeable flavour to vegetables, and this is found to be the case with those cultivated in the Chinese gardens.

The whole subject is one which may well occupy the attention of English agriculturalists. . . . We could not, indeed, adopt the almost primitive plan of the Chinese; still, stone or cemented cess-pools, which should receive the drainage of both houses and stables, might, by degrees, be introduced into every well-regulated establishment . . .

It is calculated that from the city of London alone there falls into the Thames a million pounds sterling per annum . . . this same investment of a million a-year, instead of regenerating our fields, returns to us for interest the threat, at least, of death to the thousands who are compelled to inhale the poisonous gases which escape, it will be allowed that the Chinese have something to say for their primitive, simple, effective, and yet very offensive method of getting rid of the nuisance.

3) *The condition of the people: Shantung, 1835*
(W.H. Medhurst, *China: Its State and Prospects*, pp. 451–4)
The temporal condition of the natives of Shan-tung, seemed generally good. We witnessed nothing of that squalid poverty and deep distress, to be met with in other parts of the empire. The men were, for the most part, robust and well-fed, hearty and hard-working; while no want, so far as we could perceive, prevailed. We saw no beggars, and few ragged people; their clothing commonly consisted of cottons, sometimes doubled, and not unfrequently quilted; most of them wore shoes and stockings, and many had more jackets than one . . .

The women were not so good-looking as the men; some were ugly, almost all ordinary, and scarcely any handsome. They were pale-faced and sickly in general, and seldom exhibited the ruddy complexion observable in the other sex . . . some of them are scarcely able to walk at all, and are obliged either to use sticks to support them, or to lean on a servant, in order to move along the streets. The poorer sort, however, may be seen working in the fields . . .

The dwellings . . . are mostly built of granite, but occasionally of mud; while the roofs are frequently tiled, but more generally thatched. Some are plastered and white-washed, and rather tastefully fitted up; the dwellings of the poorer sort, however, stand forth in all their native and rude simplicity. The majority of the houses are about thirty feet long, ten wide, and eight high. A door occupies the centre of the front, and a window each side. Near the doorway, there are frequently seen two blocks of granite, projecting a little from the wall, with loopholes in them, which are used for tying up cattle, whilst feeding. Some houses are double, having a front and back range of buildings, but we saw few that were two stories high. The streets are from ten to twenty feet wide, running parallel to each other, crossed by narrow lanes . . . [. . .]

The ground is well cultivated, wherever it is capable of culture, and the sterility of the soil is improved by the attention that is paid to stercoration. Almost every person met with in the fields, is provided with a hand-basket and a rake, with which he collects the dung of all the cattle in the way, and carefully conveying it home, deposits it on the dung-hills, at the entrance of every village, where the manure is heaped up and ripened for use. The productions of the soil are, beans, in great quantities; millet, of various kinds; buckwheat, of a poor quality; rice, and wheat. The fields are not fenced off by hedges, but divided by small grassy ridges, sufficient to enable each man to know his own: and the houses are collected together in villages, either for defence or company. The cattle to be met with are, a small kind of oxen, horses of a diminutive size, asses in abundance, and some mules. Shaggy-haired goats were seen, but no sheep. . . . The domestic animals are never left to graze at pleasure, but tethered to a string, are removed from one place to another, when the grass is consumed. No venomous or wild beasts, of any kind, were seen, neither did we hear of any; but birds were espied, in great numbers, some of which being very tame, allowed us to come near them, without flying away.

The poor people who pursue, from youth to old age, the same monotonous round of toils, for a subsistence, never see nor hear anything of the world around them. Improvements in the useful arts and sciences, and an increase of the conveniences of life are not known among them. In the place where their fathers lived and died, they toil and pass away, to be succeeded by another generation in the same manner. The towns, and even the villages, which are noted in the old maps, we found as delineated; unchanged, except by decay, and unimproved in any respect. The people possess few of the comforts of life; neither table, chair, nor any article of furniture, was to be seen in the houses of the poorer classes. No prospect of amelioration for them appears, but in the liberalizing and happy influence of Christianity . . .

4) *Coloured green teas*
(R. Fortune, *A Journey to the Tea Countries*, pp. 92–4)
In my former work I offered some remarks upon the preference which many persons in Europe and in America have for *coloured* green teas, and I will now give a 'full and particular account' of the colouring process as practised in the Hwuy-chow green-tea country upon those

teas which are destined for the foreign market. Having noted down the process carefully at the time, I will extract verbatim from my notebook:-

'The superintendent of the workmen managed the colouring part of the process himself. Having procured a portion of Prussian blue, he threw it into a porcelain bowl, not unlike a chemist's mortar, and crushed it into a very fine powder. At the same time a quantity of gypsum was produced and burned in the charcoal fires which were then roasting the teas. . . . The gypsum, having been taken out of the fire after a certain time had elapsed, readily crumbled down and was reduced to powder in the mortar. These two substances . . . were then mixed together in the proportion of four parts of gypsum to three parts of Prussian blue . . .

'This colouring matter was applied to the teas during the last process of roasting. About five minutes before the tea was removed from the pans – the time being regulated by the burning of a joss-stick – the superintendent took a small porcelain spoon, and with it he scattered a portion of the colouring matter over the leaves in each pan. The workmen then turned the leaves rapidly round with both hands, in order that the colour might be equally diffused.

'During this part of the operation the hands of the workmen were quite blue. I could not help thinking that if any green-tea drinkers had been present during the operation their taste would have been corrected, and, I may be allowed to add, improved. It seems perfectly ridiculous that a civilised people should prefer these dyed teas to those of a natural green. No wonder that the Chinese consider the natives of the west to be a race of 'barbarians'.

'One day an English gentleman in Shanghae, being in conversation with some Chinese from the green-tea country, asked them what reasons they had for dyeing the tea. . . . They acknowledged that tea was much better when prepared without having any such ingredients mixed with it, and that they never drank dyed teas themselves, but justly remarked that, as foreigners seemed to prefer having a mixture of Prussian blue and gypsum with their tea, to make it look uniform and pretty, and as these ingredients were cheap enough, the Chinese had no objection to supply them, especially as such teas always fetched a higher price!

'I took some trouble to ascertain precisely the quantity of colouring matter used in the process of dyeing green teas . . . to show green-tea drinkers in England, and more particularly in the United States of America, what quantity of Prussian blue and gypsum they imbibe in the course of one year. To $14\frac{1}{2}$ lbs. of tea were applied 8 mace $2\frac{1}{2}$ candareens of colouring matter, or rather more than an ounce. In every hundred pounds of coloured green tea consumed in England or America, the consumer actually drinks more than half a pound of Prussian blue and gypsum! And yet, tell the drinkers of this coloured tea that the Chinese eat cats, dogs, and rats, and they will hold up their hands in amazement, and pity the poor celestials!'

5) *Silk-throwing*
(J.R. Scarth, *Twelve Years in China*, p. 19)

In the temple attached to the pagoda at Ningpo, and also in several other large temples at Foo-chow and elsewhere, silk-throwing is carried on. The process would astonish a Macclesfield throwster. The silk is hung in long lines from one end of the temple to the other, the end of the threads hanging towards the ground from a wooden framework. To the threads is attached a bullet-shaped weight, with a small iron pin to which the silk is fastened. The people employed take in each hand a flat piece of wood, something like but rather larger than the castanets boys play with in England. With the fingers of one hand at the wrist of the other, one piece of wood is pushed sharply forward, and the other drawn back. The bullet, being between the two, has thus a rapid rotatory motion given to it. It spins round for a long time, and twists the silk attached to it; but it does it too tightly for European notions, and the thrown silk brings a better price when the twist is less close.

6) *Insect white wax*
(A. Hosie, *Three Years in Western China*, pp. 192–8)

In the valley, which is about 5000 feet above the level of the sea, and on the hills which bound it, there is one very prominent tree, called by the Chinese of that region the *Ch'ung shu*, or 'Insect Tree'. . . . It is an evergreen with leaves springing in pairs from the branches. They are thick, dark-green, glossy, ovate, and pointed. In the end of May and beginning of June, the tree bears clusters of small white flowers, which are succeeded by fruit of a dark purple colour. From the specimens of the tree which I forwarded to Kew Gardens, the authorities there have come to the conclusion that it is *Ligustrum lucidum*, or large-leaved privet.

In the month of March 1883, I passed through the Chien-chang valley; but, knowing that Mr. Baber had already furnished a report on the subject of white wax, I confined myself to a mere cursory examination of the insect tree. In that month, however, I found attached to the bark of the boughs and twigs, numerous brown pea-shaped excrescences. The larger excrescences or scales were readily detachable, and, when opened, presented either a whitey-brown pulpy mass, or a crowd of minute animals like flour, whose movements were only just perceptible to the naked eye.

In the months of May and June 1884, when I was called upon for more detailed information on the subject, I had the opportunity of examining these scales and their contents . . . in the neighbourhood of Ch'ung-k'ing . . . I plucked the scales from the trees . . . and on opening them (they are very brittle) I found a swarm of brown creatures, crawling about, each provided with six legs and a pair of *antennae*. Each of these moving creatures was a white wax insect – the *coccus pe-la* of Westwood. [. . .]

On emerging from the scales, the insects creep rapidly up the branches to the leaves, among which they nestle for a period of thirteen days. They then descend to the branches and twigs, on which they take up their positions, the females, doubtless, to provide for a continuation of the race by developing scales in which to deposit their eggs, and the males to excrete the substance known as white wax . . .

The wax first appears as a white coating on the under sides of the boughs and twigs, and resembles very much sulphate of quinine, or a covering of snow. It gradually spreads over the whole branch, and attains, after three months, a thickness of about a quarter of an inch.

7) *Emigration from the districts around Foochow*
(C. Gutzlaff, *Journal of Three Voyages*, pp. 165–7)
All the districts belonging to Fuh-chow-Foo . . . send forth a great number of colonists, who spare neither danger or toil to gain a scanty livelihood in their foreign homes. A part of their hard earnings is annually remitted to their kindred who are left in their native land; and it is astonishing to see what hardships they will suffer, to procure and send home this pittance. A man of tried honesty is appointed to collect

the individual subscriptions of the emigrants, who also engages to go home with them, and there make an equitable distribution to the donees. The subscriptions are regularly noted down, and a certain per centage paid to this commissioner. . . . On arriving at his native shores, he is welcomed by all those who are anxiously waiting for this supply. The amount of these remittances is often large, and there are instances where junks have taken on board more than sixty thousand dollars for this purpose . . .

The condition of the emigrants in general, on their arrival in a foreign country, is most miserable, without clothing, or money for one day's subsistence. Sometimes they have not money enough to pay their passage from home (six or twelve dollars,) and they become bondmen to any body who pays this sum for them, or fall a prey to extortioners, who claim their services for more than a year. The junks which transport them in great numbers, remind one of an African slaver. The deck is filled with them, and there the poor wretches are exposed to the inclemency of the weather and without any shelter, for the cargo fills the junk below. Their food consists of dry rice and an allowance of water; but when the passages are very long, there is often a want of both, and many of them actually starve to death.

8) *Emigration from Amoy*
(*Correspondence with the Superintendent of British Trade*, pp. 19–20)

Acting-Consul Backhouse's Answers to Queries.

1. *Q*. HAS any emigration taken place within the last few years from the port of Amoy? If so, to what extent? – *A*. In 1847, 632 coolies went to Cuba; in 1848, 120 to Sydney; 1849, 280 to Sydney; 1850, 422 to Sydney; 1851, 1,438 to Sydney, and 200 to Honoluhu; and in 1852, 478 to Sydney, 101 to Honoluhu, 404 to Peru, 465 to Demerara, and 300 to Cuba; making a total of 4,840 coolies.
2. *Q*. Is the emigration from Amoy sanctioned or connived at by the local authorities? Are any obstacles thrown in the way of intending emigrants? – *A*. Tacitly sanctioned.
3. *Q*. Are the inhabitants of the districts adjoining to Amoy, in your opinion, well fitted for labour in a tropical climate like that of the West Indies? – *A*. Yes.

4. *Q.* What is the average rate of pay per diem for agricultural labour in and near Amoy? – *A.* For a permanent engagement, from 25 to 45 cash per diem, with food. For job work, 75 to 100 cash per diem, without food.

5. *Q.* What is the general character of the people of Amoy as regards industry and capacity of labour? – *A.* Good.

6. *Q.* In the event of an emigration taking place on a large scale, is it likely that men of respectable character and industrious habits would join it, or only the refuse of the population? – *A.* None but the destitute will go to an unknown country; but a deserving man in such circumstances will emigrate as freely as a worthless character.

7. *Q.* In the same event, is it likely that emigrants would take with them their families, and settle altogether out of China, or would they go alone, and with a view of returning? – *A.* Under any circumstances Chinamen would not be likely to remove their families from China.

8. *Q.* What would be the expense, at present rates, of shipping male adult emigrants for the West Indies *viâ* Cape Horn, per man? – *A.* 17 *l.* per man; vessels always go round the Cape of Good Hope.

9. *Q.* Would emigrants going out enter into contracts pledging themselves to work at certain rates for the same parties; or, in your judgment, would it be more desirable to leave them wholly free and unfettered? – *A.* Coolies always enter into contracts previous to starting. I consider it would be inexpedient for a different course to be pursued.

10. *Q.* What would be the average time required for a passage from Amoy to the West Indies? – *A.* About $4\frac{1}{2}$ months.

11. *Q.* State generally any facts bearing on the question of Chinese emigration to the West Indies which may occur to you as important, and which are not mentioned in the preceding queries. – *A.* No observations to make.

(Signed)
J. BACKHOUSE.

9) *Report on trade of Chefoo for the year 1877*
(*Commercial Reports by Her Majesty's Consuls in China: 1877*, pp. 36–7)
When ... we find that during a year of such scarcity as has not been equalled since the port was opened to foreign trade, the consumption

of Manchester goods has fallen so little below the average, we are justified in saying that the consumers of these goods are people above the class directly affected by the famine.

This only bears out what other considerations point to. The population of the whole of this province is generally put down at about 25,000,000, and assuming that the whole of the western half is supplied from Chinkiang viâ the Grand Canal, there still remains the eastern half, which, bad as the roads are, must find it cheaper to come here to buy than to go anywhere else. Take it that there are only 10,000,000 that draw their supplies from Chefoo, or say 2,000,000 families, a consumption of 700,000 pieces only gives each family about 15 yards a-year. I cannot say what the actual quantity used by a family may be, but when it is recollected that the whole of their clothing, upper as well as under, is cotton, and nothing but cotton (with the exception of the few who can afford to wear silk), it will be seen that it must be many times that quantity. The rest of their clothing is home-made, and the reason why they prefer it is simply because it is more economical. Yard for yard, the native-made stuff is dearer, but when it comes to washing, the durability of the latter becomes at once apparent. A coat made of native-woven cotton will outlast two or three of those made from the ordinary Manchester fabrics.

. . . So long as labour is a drug in the market, and half the people in the country are idle for a great part of the year, so long will hand looms continue to supply the wants of each household. So long as an able-bodied man's wages is only 6d. a-day, so long will the luxuries of Manchester be utterly beyond his reach.

10) *An internal customs station on the West River*
(A.R. Colquhoun, *Across Chrysê*, I, p. 56)
Every day we passed one or two Lekim, or Customs stations, so that the cost of goods must rapidly increase with the distance they have to be carried. The fact is, trade is paralysed by these Customs 'barriers'. No trade could be created in the face of such difficulties. These stations generally consist of one large, flat-bottomed boat, on which is erected the T'ing, or office of the petty official in charge, and alongside is the cook-house, on another boat. They are both curious-looking establishments.

It was amusing to notice the faces of the boatmen when we came near one of these stations; their evident anxiety, their affected indifference, the eagerness with which they imparted the intelligence that they had English mandarins on board, and last, but not least, the look of relief when they were once well away. Why all this anxiety to 'rush' these stations? – because, doubtless, they were smuggling salt!

11)*Tenure of land in China*
(G. Jamieson, 'Tenure of Land in China', pp. 106–7)

From REV. J.F. JOHNSON
American Presbyterian Mission, Hangchow, Chêkiang.

The agricultural holdings or farms here vary in size from 3 or 4 to 20 or 30 mow, as a general thing. The average size is probably 12 or 15 mow.

Of the cultivators, I was told that $\frac{2}{3}$, perhaps $\frac{1}{2}$, are owners of the land; the rest, leasers or renters. One able-bodied, expert workman is supposed to tend 6 mow. Hired labour is much used, and at rates like these: for a day's work, from 120 to 160 cash; for a month's, from 2,400 to 3,000 cash; boys get about 1,000 cash a month; and in every case the labourer is fed by the employer. By a mutual-help system many farmers avoid the necessity of employing hired help.

The landlord is paid $\frac{1}{3}$ of the produce as rent. In our *hien* the largest farm is about 200 mow; in our *foo* there are a few men who hold 1,000 mow or more, but perhaps none who have as much as 10,000 mow.

The average yield per mow varies with the soil and with the year. Good land will ordinarily yield 2 tan (piculs) of hulled rice; poor land, perhaps 1 tan. . . . Barley or wheat is but little grown here. The farmer gets from $1.70 to $2 a tan for his rice, the retail price of which is from 240 to 320 cash a *tou*.

Land tax is paid in silver in the 5th moon, at the rate of 1 tael for 7 mow; in the 11th moon in rice, at the rate of 6.08 shing a mow. And these taxes are paid at the Yamêns and granaries of the different hiens. Many of the farmers pay tax with a bad grace; they often give tax-collectors and townsmen a piece of their mind upon the slightest provocation.

People here speak of the land of the Shaohing plain as unusually productive.

Many small farmers engage in other businesses during their leisure from farm work.

One of my informants says, that the total land tax for a year varies between 400 and 1,000 cash a mow, according to the quality of the land.

There is but little arable land near us that does not yield at least two or three different crops a year.

April 14th, 1888

12) *A journey to examine the coal mines west of Peking, 1863*
(R. Pumpelly, 'A Journey in Northern China', p. 467)
Alarmed at the idea of having to pay from fifteen to twenty dollars a ton for English coal, and knowing that they had themselves large deposits of this mineral, they decided to search for desirable fuel among their own mines.

The arrangements were made over a lunch at the Tsung-li-yamun, with the officers of the Board of Foreign Affairs. The interview, which was very friendly, brought out some curious ideas with regard to geology. Among these was the belief in the growth of coal in abandoned mines: everything was produced by the co-action of yin and yang, force and matter, the active and passive, male and female principles in nature, and where surrounding conditions had once favored the production of coal, why should they not always favor it? But at the same time they objected to extensive mining, on the ground that it would exhaust the store on which future generations would be dependent; an inconsistency in reasoning which they got over by saying that the rate of growth of new coal is not known. Another objection to extensive mining was the danger of litigation from trespass, and one of the officers immediately proceeded to give a long and romantic story of a desperate subterranean battle which had raged for days between the forces of two mines which had suddenly become connected under ground; an encounter in which the participants were mutually ex-terminated.

It was agreed that three mandarins, two civil, and one military, should go with me. The question having arisen as to how my name could be intelligibly written in Chinese, Tung-Ta-jin selected for the first syllable the word Pang, as the nearest approach offered by the language, and wrote it for me on a card in a character in which the principal element was the sign of a dragon; did they think there might be some connection between the intended approach to foreign innovations and the clutches of this terrific monster?

13) *The Ping-Tu Gold Mine, Shantung*
(E. Clark, 'Notes on the Progress of Mining in China', pp. 579–80)
The mines have been worked by the Chinese for a number of years. Under European auspices and the superintendence of Mr. H.M. Beecher, of England, the systematic development of the mine at Ping-Tu was begun in 1886, and a twenty-stamp mill made by the Union Iron Works, of San Francisco, with eight Frue vanners and eight Hendy concentrators, was erected. After the mill was in operation, the hoisting-arrangements were found inadequate to keep it supplied with ore, and a new fifty-thousand-dollar hoisting-plant, with Ingersoll rock-drills, was erected under the superintendence of Colonel Ellsworth, of San Francisco.

The upper portion of the vein was quite rich. The writer was informed that the first clean-up amounted to $10,000. When in full operation the mine had a staff of twelve Americans, a very large Chinese clerical force, with its numerous servants, and the usual crowded labor underground and on the surface. As the mine increased in depth, the ore carried less free gold and more sulphurets, and the amount of amalgam that could be scraped from the plates rapidly decreased. The foreign employees, always more or less dissatisfied with an unprofitable mine, gradually left, and their places were filled with Chinese who had but imperfect knowledge of amalgamation and the general working of a stamp-mill. In the fall of 1889 supplies fell short, and, with the failure to receive coal, the mine-pumps were stopped, and the workings allowed to fill with water.

14) *The introduction of the telegraph*
(W.A.P. Martin, *A Cycle of Cathay*, pp. 299–300)
Besides teaching English to my ten pupils, I gave them lessons in the use and management of the telegraph. With a view to the introduction of that wonderful invention, I had myself taken lessons in Philadelphia; and I had brought with me, at my own expense, two sets of instruments, one on the Morse system, the other with an alphabetic

dial-plate, easy to learn and striking to the eye. Before taking charge of this class I invited the Yamen to send officials to my house to witness experiments. Prince Kung deputed the four Chinese who were aiding me in the revision of Wheaton. During the performance they looked on without giving any sign of intelligence or interest; one of them, a Hanlin, or academician, observed contemptuously that 'China had been a great empire for four thousand years without the telegraph.' On being shown a few toys they were delighted, spending much time in catching magnetic fish and in leading or chasing magnetic geese, chuckling all the while over the novelty of the sport. In letters they were men, in science children.

NOTE

1. Du Halde, *A Description of the Empire of China*, I, p. 314.

THE MILITARY

Many western writers, coming from countries where military or naval power was a matter of pride, where military valour was an esteemed quality, and where the advance of military technology was regarded as a measure of progress, found it difficult to gauge China's military potential. Inevitably the yardstick was a comparison with the military in the west, and by the beginning of the nineteenth century, that comparison was almost entirely derogatory to China (1).

The suspicion of China's military inefficiency was fully confirmed during the Opium War. Chinese troops were no match for British forces on land and British naval forces, aided by the *Nemesis*, overwhelmed any opposition the Chinese could muster at sea. The *Nemesis* was the first iron steam vessel to reach China. She displaced about seven hundred tons and was armed with two 32-pounder guns. As she drew only 6 feet of water she could operate in the shallow creeks of the Canton estuary. With her watertight bulkheads she was in effect invulnerable to the Chinese and could cause immense destruction to their ships, as was demonstrated in the naval operations near Canton in May 1841. The account of this operation also described an early manifestation of Chinese nationalism. The fleet of fire-ships had been organized, not by the government, but by the gentry from the villages north of Canton (2). Another interesting description of the military actions of the Opium War is that of Lt. John Ouchterlony, who noted the desperate resistance offered by a Manchu garrison (3).

The impression of China's helplessness was confirmed by the *Arrow* war of 1856–60. In December 1857, Elgin, the British Plenipotentiary and a man of acute sensibilities, confided his feelings to his journal. Yeh Ming-ch'en, the Governor-General, had failed to respond to his ultimatum, and he now concluded sadly that he had to authorize an assault on Canton, the entry to which had been disputed since the Opium War (4).

The question arose: why were the Chinese unable to defend themselves? Was it because they lacked military valour? In the *Arrow* war, two engagements occurred at the Taku forts, which defended the approaches to Tientsin. These conflicts were used as evidence on the subject of Chinese and Manchu bravery. In 1858, according to the Marquis de Moges, attaché to the French mission, who visited the forts the day after their capture, the garrison was reasonably well supplied, albeit with obsolete weapons. A Manchu officer had responded bravely, but the officials had been irresolute, and the rank and file had no stomach for a fight, and so the forts were overwhelmed (5). In 1860 the forts were again attacked and again defended with resolution, but for Robert Swinhoe, Staff Interpreter to General Sir Hope Grant, this was only the bravery of the desperate (6). A different perspective on the qualities of Chinese soldiers was offered by their conduct in the ranks of the western-officered Ever-Victorious Army (7).

At the beginning of the nineteenth century, there were two regular military forces in China: the Manchu Banner troops, used to garrison key points throughout the country, and the Chinese Army of the Green Standard, employed to maintain law and order. Both of these formations had become inefficient, and when tested by the widespread outbreak of rebellion, the dynasty had to permit the formation of a new type of force, the regional army, raised with gentry assistance and controlled by regional officials. It was these forces which first made extensive use of western weapons and adopted western drill. To equip these forces China embarked on a programme of 'self-strengthening' and established modern arsenals and shipyards, sometimes with British and French assistance. China's endeavours in this direction led to a fresh appreciation of her military capacity (8).

British soldiers in China could now study conditions in the Chinese armed forces at close quarters, and could compare their conduct with that of western troops (9). The Army of the Green Standard fought in the Sino-French War of 1883–5, and its performance in Tongking, facing some of France's best soldiers, gave a better impression of the fighting ability of the Chinese (10).

However, the inadequacy of China's attempt at 'self-strengthening' was mercilessly exposed in the Sino-Japanese War of 1894–5 and this failure raised fundamental questions about the capacity of imperial

China to survive. Westerners began to predict that the Empire would disintegrate and this seemed even more probable after the western powers and Japan had joined in a scramble for concessions, which, by the end of the century, had led to large parts of China falling into spheres of influence of the powers. Among those who warned of China's peril was Sir Robert Hart, head of the Imperial Maritime Service (11).

After the Sino-Japanese War, an effort was made to shore up the dynasty by establishing a genuine modern army. Lord Charles Beresford, a naval man, had been sent to China to advise on what protection the Chinese government could provide for British enterprises. He commented on China's military capacity, and in particular on the army under the command of Yüan Shih-k'ai, who was to play the key role in the 1911 revolution. Beresford was pessimistic about China's chance of survival. He entitled his report *The Break-up of China*, which he described as 'an event that has no parallel in history', and went on to say that 'the maintenance of the Chinese Empire is essential to the honour as well as the interests of the Anglo-Saxon race' (12). His pessimism was echoed by Major A.E.J. Sutherland, of the 1st Argyll and Sutherland Highlanders, a former military attaché with the Chinese army, who described China's vaunted military power as 'imaginary strength', and likely to remain as such unless placed under European tutelage (13).

1) *Chinese soldiers*
(H. Ellis, *Journal of the Proceedings of the Late Embassy to China*, pp. 137–8)
A halt of our boat, opposite a party of soldiers, drawn out to do honour to the Embassador, gave me an opportunity of examining them with a little attention. They were, to use a military phrase, of all arms – matchlocks, bows and arrows, swords, shields, and quilted breastplates. Their bow is shaped like the Persian bow, that is, not a continued arch; but, unlike the latter, it requires little strength to draw them: their arrows are deeply feathered, more than three feet long, with a pointed blade at the end not barbed. Chinese matchlocks are the worst that I have ever seen; originally of ill construction, they are kept in such bad order, that they must become perfectly useless. The swords are short and well-shaped, being slightly curved, and do not

seem bad weapons. The bowstring rests against the thumb, and for that purpose a broad ring of bone, or some hard substance, is worn to protect the skin. The appearance of the strangely drest soldiers already mentioned, who may be called the monsters of the imperial guard, is most ludicrous: the colours of the dress are such as I before described; the dress itself is divided into a loose jacket and trowsers: some of the party had a coloured cloth wrapped like a scanty clout round their heads: they hold their capacious shields in front, close to their breasts, and allow a few inches of their rusty blade to appear above it. The principal officer on duty wore a blue button. Such is the superiority of civil over military rank in China, that a civil Mandarin with a white button often takes precedence of the military coral.

2) *The* Nemesis *in action*
(W.D. Bernard, *The Nemesis in China*, pp. 168–9)
Just when all opposition at the Shameen battery had been overcome, an unlooked-for opportunity occurred of rendering signal service, by the discovery of the principle rendezvous of all the fire-rafts and men-of-war junks. . . . The first thing which led to the discovery was the suspicious appearance of a large war-junk, which suddenly came out from behind a point of land some way above the fort. Having fired one or two distant shots, she again withdrew out of sight.

The Nemesis instantly proceeded in search of the expected prize, accompanied by Captain Herbert. . . . The junk again stole out from her hiding-place, but, the moment she observed the steamer coming towards her, she made off in all haste up a large creek, which turned round to the northward. About a mile or less within this passage, the whole Chinese fleet of war-junks, fire-rafts, boats, &c., was suddenly descried, to the number, probably, of more than a hundred. This was an exciting moment. The Chinese were thrown into the utmost consternation by the sudden approach of the steamer; and the more numerous were the junks and craft of all kinds, the greater was the confusion into which they were thrown. Every shot now told upon the confused mass. The Chinese ran most of their boats ashore, in order to make their own escape; others tried to make their way up the creek, each striving to pass the other. Suddenly a small masked battery opened fire upon the steamer; but a few round shot, followed by grape, drove the Chinese from their guns, and served to disperse a small body of troops, who were drawn up in the rear. The water soon became too shallow for the steamer to proceed further, and she, therefore, came to anchor. . . . About 50 boats were found filled with combustibles, and were joined eight or nine together, having been destined to drift down with the tide upon our vessels. Many of the junks had troops on board, from distant parts of the empire, intended for the relief of the city.

The scene was extremely animating; numbers of the Chinese were scrambling ashore, or clinging to fragments of their boats or spars. . . . Some of the junks were burnt, and others blown up, but the precaution was taken to examine carefully every one of them before it was set on fire, in order to rescue any of the panic-stricken Chinese who might be trying to find concealment in it. But, in spite of this precaution, the structure of the junks afforded so many little hiding-places for the terrified Chinese, that, as the fires gradually burnt more briskly . . . several poor fellows were observed to rush up from below, and then, unable to support the heat upon deck, to jump desperately overboard. Some of these swam easily on shore; others, who could not swim, remained clinging to the outside of the junk, or to the rudder, until the heat became insupportable, or the vessel itself blew up. In this way, some few necessarily perished, for it was not possible to save them all. . . . Thus, in the short space of three hours, 43 war-junks were blown up, and 32 fire-rafts destroyed, besides smaller boats.

3) *The Manchu garrison at Chapu*
(J. Ouchterlony, *The Chinese War*, pp. 286–7)

. . . As this place afforded the first opportunity which the expedition had enjoyed of examining that remarkable system of living apart from the Chinese, pursued by the Tartars in all towns where they have adopted permanent residences, much interest was excited by the investigation of the buildings included in what was styled the 'Tartar city'. It was found to contain, besides magazines for arms, powder, saltpetre, and grain, and a foundry upon a small scale, several exceedingly commodious ranges of barracks, consisting of rows of small houses in streets, with cooking-houses, and small plots of ground attached to every two, with guard-houses and parade-grounds in their vicinity, and the whole united in a manner which proved that the discipline maintained (as the sole foundation of the throne of the Mant-chow dynasty) would suffer but little by comparison with that of our more refined armies of Europe.

Miserable, however, was the spectacle presented by the interior of most of the better class of houses in the 'Tartar city', on the entrance of our troops: strewed on the floors, or suspended from the rafters, were to be seen the bodies of women and young children, bloody from the wounds by which their lives had been cut short, or swollen and blackened by the effects of poison. Impelled by the same feeling of exclusiveness and pride which characterizes their habits of life as well as of government, it seems that the Tartars of Chapoo, even when defeated . . . never for a moment contemplated removing their families from the town, and escaping beyond our pursuit, but, with a stern resolution to maintain to the last the inviolability of their homes, (which, though we decry it as barbarian, must yet command a share of our respect,) preferred staining them with their blood, to surviving to abandon them to the polluting touch and presence of the invader.

4) *Canton at Elgin's Mercy*
(*Letters and Journals of James, Eighth Earl of Elgin*, p. 212)
December 22nd. – On the afternoon of the 20th, I got into a gunboat with Commodore Elliot . . . and we actually steamed past the city of Canton, along the whole front, within pistol-shot of the town. A line of English men-of-war are now anchored there in front of the town. I never felt so ashamed of myself in my life, and Elliot remarked that the trip seemed to have made me sad. There we were, accumulating the means of destruction under the very eyes, and within the reach, of a population of about 1,000,000 people, against whom these means of destruction were to be employed! 'Yes,' I said to Elliot, 'I am sad, because when I look at that town, I feel that I am earning for myself a place in the Litany, immediately after "plague, pestilence, and famine".' I believe however that, as far as I am concerned, it was impossible for me to do otherwise than as I have done. I could not have abandoned the demand to enter the city after what happened last winter, without compromising our position in China altogether, and opening the way to calamities even greater than those now before us. I made my demands on Yeh as moderate as I could, so as to give him a chance of accepting; although, if he had accepted, I knew that I should have brought on my head the imprecations both of the navy and army and of the civilians, the time being given by the missionaries and the women. And now Yeh having refused, I shall do whatever I can

possibly do to secure the adoption of plans of attack, &c., which will lead to the least destruction of life and property.

5) *Bravery of a Manchu colonel*
(Marquis de Moges, *Recollections of Baron Gros's Embassy*, pp. 213–14)
At four o'clock in the morning the bugle was sounded; every one, stiff with a hard bed on the hard ground, was glad to be up and to return to duty. There was a certain amount of poetry in the scene at daybreak. The rising sun, the tall waving reeds, the noisy flight of the gulls and sea-fowl, produced an impression altogether new. We explored all parts of the camp. There were lying about fragments of broken bows, arrows, gunpowder soaked in water, gingalls, matchlocks, cannons, banners, tents, heaps of balls, case-shot, and arms of every kind. It was evident that the commander of the fort had spared no precautions. Poor man! he lay himself stark and stiff among the ruins. When he saw that his men had ceased to fire, and that the foreign seamen were clambering over the ramparts, he could not survive his defeat. He threw himself on his knees at the brink of the ditch, and, with his long sword, cut a fatal gash right across his throat, before our sailors had the presence of mind to rush in and prevent him. He died immediately. This was Tchen, the Mantchoo colonel, whom we had received on board, and to whom we would have been delighted to have given a warm and friendly reception. We took a walk several times towards the village of Ta-kou. The space which separates the town from the camp was literally covered with conical hats, which the Chinese warriors had dropped in the hurry of their flight. We saw the corpses of two or three Chinese soldiers with their heads cut open and their hands tied behind their backs, whom the mandarins had caused to be executed while they remained themselves at their posts, for having run off a little sooner than their commanders.

6) *Defence of Taku forts*
(R. Swinhoe, *Narrative of the North China Campaign*, pp. 138–9)
The Tartars undoubtedly fought like brave men, hurling down all kind of uncouth missiles at the storming party; and when our troops had effected an entrance, every inch of the ground inside the fort was disputed. But I cannot help thinking that the bravery of the enemy was a good deal due to the peculiarity of their circumstances. By blocking

us out, they had blocked themselves in, and so fell into a complete trap, from which there was no hope of escape. They therefore exerted their utmost to keep out their assailants; but when once in, they could hardly expect quarter from the excited state of the men's blood. There was, therefore, no alternative but to fight hard for their lives. Thus, *magnis componere parva*, that domestic nuisance the house-rat, if allowed a chance of escape, is only too glad to avail itself of it; but if boxed up with a terrier in a pit, tries hard to bite the jaws that are about to inflict his death-wound.

The true native cowardice of the race evinced itself in the submissive conduct of the second north fort garrison and subsequent unconditional surrender of the southern forts, notwithstanding the strength of their position and the heavy armament they contained.

The fearless conduct, however, of the Cantonese coolies in our lines excited considerable admiration. They seemed to enjoy the fun, and shouted with glee at every good shot that carried a murderous mission, no matter whether it committed havoc among the enemy, or bowled over our unfortunate fellows. . . . All this, it will be argued, shows no lack of pluck in the Chinese character when opportunity is given for its demonstration; but we must not forget that the people from whom these corps were taken were mostly thieves or pirates hardened to deeds of blood, and depending largely on such acts for their maintenance.

7) *The qualities of the Chinese soldier*
(A. Wilson, *The 'Ever-Victorious Army'*, pp. 268–9)
As the Chinese would be less expensive, and not less efficient, than English soldiers for service in India, it is of importance to note their physical characteristics. The old notion is pretty well got rid of, that they are at all a cowardly people when properly paid and efficiently led; while the regularity and order of their habits, which dispose them to peace in ordinary times, give place to a daring bordering upon recklessness in time of war. Their intelligence and capacity for remembering facts make them well fitted for use in modern warfare, as do also the coolness and calmness of their disposition. Physically they are on an average not so strong as Europeans, but considerably more so than most of the other races of the East; and on a cheap diet of rice, vegetables, salt fish, and pork, they can go through a vast amount of

fatigue, whether in a temperate climate or in a tropical one, where Europeans are ill-fitted for exertion. Their wants are few; they have no caste prejudices, and hardly any appetite for intoxicating liquors. Being of a lymphatic or lymphatic-bilious temperament, they enjoy a remarkable immunity from inflammatory disease, and the tubercular diathesis is little known amongst them.

8) *The Chinese instructed on the building of steamships*
(P. Giquel, *The Foochow Arsenal*, p. 26)
The Foundry. – The head-workmen, Robeson and Rivasseau, are at the present moment in charge, the one of the iron foundry, the other of the brass foundry. . . . Twenty-one workmen and apprentices for the iron foundry, and five for the brass foundry, fulfil the conditions of the contract. Annexed I send the list of them to Your Excellency. After having carefully examined them on the reading of the plans, and the working of the various parts of an engine, I questioned them as to the practical difficulties of their business. For example, I asked them what mixtures of sand ought to be used according to the nature of the pieces that had to be cast . . . how the patterns ought to be arranged in the moulds for certain difficult pieces; what precautions should be taken in order that the gas might be able to escape from the casting, and under what conditions the casting ought to be made. After this examination had taken place I submitted the arrangements of that workshop to Your Excellency, and I requested that it be handed over to the Chinese workmen, and that they should be set to construct all the pieces of an engine of the new pattern, and the pieces awanting for engine No. 5, of the old pattern. The workshop was handed over by the European staff on the 3rd September, 1873; and already almost all the pieces of these two engines have been delivered to the Fitting shop; the cylinders, which may be regarded as the most difficult parts, have been cast with complete success.

9) *Chinese and British soldiers compared*
(J. Lamprey, 'The Economy of the Chinese Army', p. 421)
The Chinese soldier, like the generality of his countrymen, is by no means addicted to intemperance, the bane of the British army. Seldom indeed is it that a drunken Chinaman is met with, although they do not eschew alcoholic drink as if they were teetotallers, on the contrary they

generally take a small quantity at their meals when they can afford it. But what alcohol is to the British soldier, opium is to the Chinese soldier, and it gives almost as much trouble to their military commanders, and requires the infliction of severe punishment for its restraint, as intemperance does to our own commanding officers. The punishment usually practised by the Chinese for this offence, is to stick small arrows, a few inches in length through the lobes of the ears, and to lead the culprit about the camp for a general admonition. But we can understand how ineffectual punishment is, when we know that the desire of the opium smoker for opium, 'is like the greed of the hawk for flesh', as the Chinese describe the peculiar craving of the *habitué*.

10) *The Chinese Brave*
(J.G. Scott, 'The Chinese Brave', pp. 225–6)
Then began a terrible struggle in the narrow winding lanes between the houses. Frenchmen and Chinamen fought literally hand to hand, and the strength was not always with the white man. Many a puny Gaul was only saved by having his bayonet fixed and knowing how to use it. A big French captain, a powerful man, with a voice like a trombone, that made him known all over the army, got to hand-grips with an equally brawny Chinaman, and the Celestial had the better of the struggle. He got the Frenchman down, and was just seizing his knife to cut his foeman's head off, when the lieutenant-colonel of the regiment blew his brains out with a revolver, and the captain scrambled, bathed in blood, from beneath the dead body. The Frenchmen were in the greater numbers, and the Chinese had no notion of getting together for defence or retreat. They were killed off separately without mercy, and next day the Tongkinese *Tirailleurs* made a large pyramid of their heads.

At Chu . . . another desperate struggle took place. There the French were not so numerous and the Chinese did not allow themselves to be hemmed in. In fact, they got a company of the 111th of the line into a particularly tight place, and would have avenged the Kep slaughter if they had had any system or anyone to lead them. But it was simple indiscriminate mob-work, and before they had made up their minds what to do the artillery had found them out and time shell were bursting about their ears.

11) *A Bad Case of Humpty Dumpty*
(R. Hart to E.B. Drew, 7 April, 1895, H.B. Morse, *The International Relations of the Chinese Empire*, III, p. 50)
China's collapse has been terrible, and the comical and tragical have dovetailed all along the frontier of incident in the most heartbreaking, side-bursting fashion. Even to-day those who can, try to make their own game out of any sycee issued for expenditure and the heart of the country knows nothing of the war, and will not make allowances for defeat: thus the government will have its own difficulties in getting the people at large to believe in sacrifices made for peace, and internal trouble may appear just as the external war ends. But in fact, although it is only at a minute spot along the fringe of this big empire that the Chinese have received thrashing after thrashing, it is the shell of the egg that is cracked, and – it seems to me a bad case of Humpty Dumpty. The conditions were terrible, and those wily Japanese have played their cards – even in framing conditions – with such a mixture of civilized grace and Asiatic slyness that all the world will be on their side and applaud, and all China will wince from north to south and for a whole cycle! I am trying to get rid of an innocent impossibility which might any day become a breach of treaty and a new *casus belli*, and also of a pound of flesh plus blood stipulation which would be hard to stagger under, as well as to round off a few corners to a shape that will be easier: but I find the other party is too clever and knows both what it wants, and how to get it, too well, to allow me to hope for success. Japan wants to lead the East in war, in commerce, and in manufactures, and next century will be a hard one for the West! Everything that China should have yielded gracefully to others when asked for will now have to be yielded to Japan's hectoring: Japan will then pose and say to all creation – 'That's the way to do it, you see, and it's I that did it!'

12) *Yüan Shih-k'ai's Army*
(Lord Charles Beresford, *The Break-up of China*, pp. 271–3)
On October 27, 1898, I went to Hsiao Chan to visit General Yuan Shi Kai, and to attend a review of his troops. I stayed two days and one night with the General, and during that time I not only saw all his troops paraded and manoeuvred, but had ample opportunity to examine the equipment of all their arms. I also visited the stores, clothing, and provisions, made myself acquainted with the complement

of each regiment, and went carefully through the monthly pay-sheets of the whole army ...

The strength of the army was 7,400 men – mostly Shantung men. These and the Hunanese are reported to make the best soldiers in China. General Yuan Shi Kai is a Chinaman, and his army is composed of Chinese. The infantry were armed with Mauser rifles – German made. He had ten 6-gun batteries of artillery of different calibres, throwing from 1 lb. to 6 lb. projectiles. The cavalry were armed with lances and a Mauser infantry rifle. On parade the whole force appeared an exceptionally smart body of men of extremely fine physique.... At my request the General put them through various parade movements, and then carried out manoeuvres in the surrounding country which proved to me that both officers and men were thoroughly conversant with their duties. Their discipline was excellent. With the exception of the artillery and the Maxims, all equipment was serviceable and efficient. I suggested to the General to practically test the equipment of the artillery and Maxims by galloping them over some rough ground. The result was to prove conclusively that the equipment was useless.

I found the General most energetic and intelligent, and a well-informed and well-educated man. He is also a thoroughly patriotic Chinaman, and most loyal to the dynasty. He expressed genuine anxiety as to the future of this country, and was quite of opinion that unless she undertook some measures for her own preservation nothing could save her falling to pieces ... [...]

If all the Chinese generals were like General Yuan Shi Kai the armies and their financial arrangements would not be in the condition they are now. General Yuan Shi Kai spends the money he receives for his army as intended. He personally superintends the payment of his men's wages and the distribution of rations and clothing.

This army is the only army complete in all detail, according to European ideas, that I found in China ...

13) *China's imaginary strength*
(A.E.J. Cavendish, 'The Armed Strength (?) of China', p. 723)
It seems a libel on the human race to say that out of the manhood of 300 millions of Chinese a body of good soldiers cannot be made; and with the example of the army which has been evolved from the

Egyptian fellaheen, it may be premature to call it impossible. But China herself cannot do it; the very best human material and the most elaborate instruction would be wasted under the existing native official, who steadily resists all reform in his maladministration.

Nevertheless, the docile soldiers and sailors of China have never yet had a chance of showing under proper management what are their real capabilities; should they under European tutelage ever prove themselves in any numbers to be of real military value, the 'Yellow Terror' may not be a mere figment of the superheated brain.

TRAVELLING

For most of the nineteenth century westerners travelling in the interior of China used modes of transport unchanged by technological advance. The contrast between this and western railway comfort became increasingly apparent, and descriptions of travel make much of the quaintness and discomfort (1). Land travel in China had always been exceedingly laborious, and this was still true when the Revd Kenneth Mackenzie travelled by cart from Tientsin to Peking in 1879 (2). A more sophisticated traveller, E. Colborne Baber, was in no doubt about the psychological value of using a sedan chair (3).

River travel was always more pleasant and was widely used. Thomas Taylor Meadows had a boat specially adapted to enable him travel unrecognized on the Grand Canal. Isabella Bird, at the age of sixty-five, began the journeys which culminated in her 'truly spectacular venture' up the Yangtze valley. For the stage from Wan Hsien to Chungking she used a small houseboat, which had some comfortable amenities and a strange atmosphere – the wife of the skipper was alleged to have beaten her eldest boy to death a few months before (4).

All travellers have things to say about the accommodation they find at the end of their journeys. Western travellers in China vied with each other to describe the most disagreeable lodging they had ever encountered – again one must suppose that the contrast with conditions in Europe was now wide (5 and 6). Travellers usually subsisted on local food. In this century, the reputation of the Chinese cuisine has grown, and it is surprising to discover that a westerner of that time found little enjoyment in Chinese cooking (7 and 8).

The main topographical features of China had been identified by the Jesuits, but at the beginning of the nineteenth century the only recent descriptions of the interior of the country were those of the embassies headed by Macartney and Amherst which had been granted exceptional access. Many parts of China, away from the coast, were

---

113

unknown to Europeans and undescribed in western accounts. As the century progressed, adventurous journeys were undertaken which resulted in publications. Sometimes western interest in these unexplored areas was patently political. In 1858 and in 1860, Russia acquired from China two large tracts of territory, which were to form the Amur and Maritime provinces of the Russian empire. The man on the spot was Thomas Witlam Atkinson who had travelled extensively in the area, and who approved of the Russian acquisition (9). Atkinson's dislike of Chinese traders and his friendly feeling towards other ethnic groups was a common response among travellers. Some recognized that the culture of these non-Chinese peoples was under threat and took care to record what they had seen and heard (10 and 11).

A major motive for undertaking journeys of this kind was to identify commercial opportunities for the West. The largest prize was the opening up of an overland route from India to China. Captain Thomas W. Blakiston attempted to do this in 1860, and described his journey in *Five Months on the Yangtze*. Blakiston had to give up at P'ing-shan in Szechuan province. The journey was attempted by T.T. Cooper eight years later, but he too had to turn back 100 miles short of his objective. His account contained details of commercial activity in the area, for example of the trade in brick tea to Tibet, with suggestions on how that might be supplied from Assam. He also gave a lively description of the hardships and dangers of travel (12). Cooper reached the historic bridge over the Tatu river which, sixty years later, was the scene of one of the most famous incidents on the Long March (13).

1) *Wheelbarrows*
(Marquis de Moges, *Recollections of Baron Gros's Embassy*, pp. 280–1)
In some parts of China wheelbarrows with sails attached to them are in use. When a good breeze blows from behind, or from one side, human labour is very much lightened by this means. This fact may at first appear a traveller's tale, but it is not such. These barrows are largely used in China for purposes of locomotion. The missionaries, for the sake of economy, often prefer them to any other vehicle, in spite of the fatigue of managing them. Often while we stayed at Shang-hai and Tien-tsin we saw these singular conveyances arrive from off a journey. The wheel is placed in the middle of the machine. The traveller sits on one side, and his luggage is placed opposite to him by way of counterpoise.

2) *Travelling by cart from Tientsin to Peking*
(Mrs Bryson, *John Kenneth Mackenzie*, pp. 166–7)

We started our journey at 9 a.m., and it took us two and a half days' cart travelling to reach Peking, a distance of eighty miles. These carts are heavy, ugly, wooden contrivances, so small that only one person can conveniently sit or lie inside, for there is no seat except the floor of the cart. If, therefore, two persons travel together one has to sit on one shaft in front, while the driver occupies the other. The cartwheels are of great thickness, iron-bound, and very strongly made; an essential condition for travelling on these bad roads. The axle-tree extends fully a foot on each side beyond the cart, so that in meeting these carts you have to be careful not to come in contact with this protruding axle-tree. The interior of a cart is about five and a half feet long by three and a half feet broad, and the covered part is three and a half feet high. Having no springs, and the road being frightfully cut up with ruts, the jolting is simply awful. We line the interior with our bedding and pillows, thus making a soft cushion to lie upon; but to prevent your coming in contact with the sides of the cart you have to seize hold of the structure of the vehicle itself to prevent incessant concussions. The soil is impregnated with soda in such quantities that it is a dusty, grey, soft substance, in dry weather easily cut into ruts, and carried about by the wind. Therefore, when a slight wind is blowing you are soon completely covered with dust, which penetrates your clothes and gets into your nostrils and throat. In wet weather the roads are pretty nearly impassable; you are ploughing through mud, and getting stuck every few minutes.

3) *The advantages of using a sedan chair*
(E.C. Baber, *Travels and Researches in Western China*, pp. 1–2)

No traveller in Western China who possesses any sense of self-respect should journey without a sedan chair, not necessarily as a conveyance, but for the honour and glory of the thing. Unfurnished with this indispensable token of respectability, he is liable to be thrust aside on the highway, to be kept waiting at ferries, to be relegated to the worst inn's worst room, and generally to be treated with indignity or, what is sometimes worse, with familiarity, as a peddling footpad who, unable to gain a living in his own country, has come to subsist on China. A chair is far more effective than a passport. One may ride on pony-back, but a chair should be in attendance. I venture to attribute Baron v. Richthofen's unlucky encounter on the pass above Ch'ing-ch'i Hsien partly to his having travelled without a chair; indeed, the natives told me that, seeing him ride about the country in what appeared to them a vague and purposeless manner, they imagined him to be a fugitive from some disastrous battle. A chair is, moreover, very useful as the safest vehicle for carrying instruments, and for stowing away all those numerous odds and ends which it is troublesome to unpack frequently from trunks. The mat cushions and arm-pillows with which it is furnished make the coolest and most comfortable bed which can be wished for in hot weather, when laid upon a couple of square tables or a stratum of planks. My coolies were hired by the month, at 300 cash – about tenpence – per diem for each man.

4) *A houseboat on the Upper Yangtze*
(I. Bird, *The Yangtze Valley and Beyond*, pp. 100–1)
The boat itself was a small house-boat of about twenty tons, flat-bottomed, with one tall mast and big sail, a projecting rudder, and a steering sweep on the bow. Her 'passenger accommodation' consisted of a cabin the width of the boat, with a removable front, opening on the bow deck, where the sixteen boatmen rowed, smoked, ate, and slept round a central well in which a preternaturally industrious cook washed bowls, prepared food, cooked it, and apportioned it all day long, using a briquette fire. At night uprights and a mat roof were put up, and the toilers, after enjoying their supper, and their opium pipes at the stern, rolled themselves in wadded quilts and slept till daybreak. Passengers usually furnish this cabin, and put up curtains and photographs, and eat and sit there; but I had no superfluities, and my 'furniture' consisted only of a carrying-chair, in which it was very delightful to sit and watch the grandeurs and surprises of the river. But gradually the trackers and the skipper's family came to over run this cabin, and I constantly found the virago with her unwelcome baby girl, or a dirty, half-naked tracker in my chair, and the eight-year-old boy spent much of his time crouching in a corner out of reach of his mother's tongue and fist.

5) *A hotel at Shah-shih, on the Yangtze*
(T.T. Cooper, *Travels of a Pioneer of Commerce*, pp. 44–5)

My visitors left about 11 p.m., and I then prepared for bed. Shortly after turning in, I suddenly began to feel an uncomfortable crawling sensation in several parts of my body, accompanied by great irritation. I mentioned this to Philip, who thereupon advised me to get up, and he would see what it was. We looked, and discovered insects innumerable. This was my first experience of Chinese beds. The first shock was painful, and I hesitated to turn in again; but Philip . . . assured me that every hotel in China was the same, and if these small matters prevented me sleeping, I should have a bad time of it. I suppressed my horror as much as possible, and turned in again, but not before I had the straw mattrass, which is always provided at hotels, thrown into the court-yard. In a very short time my torments began again, sleep I could not, and I lay tossing about on the hard boards in perfect agony. At last I groaned aloud, and attracted the attention of one of my neighbours and visitors of the evening in an adjoining room, who inquired what was the matter, and on Philip informing her, she and her companions screamed with laughter. Finding sleep impossible, I got up and dressed, and sought solace in my pipe, while I sat for hours thinking over the day, and making a survey of the room. It was blackened by the tobacco smoke of ages, and smelt like a ferret cage. Dirt formed a coating several inches thick on the floor, and would have rendered living in such a place impossible, but for the ventilation admitted through a large hole in the wall which did duty as a window. Two of the four walls were mat-partitions separating our room from two other dens, in one of which an aged Celestial coughed throughout the night with asthmatic energy, while in the other were my lady visitors and their children, which little cherubs occasionally joined in a duet of screams.

6) *Chinese inns*
(A. Hosie, *Three Years in Western China*, pp. 25–6)
I have occupied hundreds of Chinese inns in the course of my travels, and I think that, on the whole, a Chinaman's own description which I found written on the wall of a room which I once tenanted in Ssŭ-ch'uan, errs on the side of leniency. In English garb it runs thus –

> Within this room you'll find the rats
> At least a goodly score,

> Three catties each they're bound to weigh,
>   Or e'en a little more;
> At night you'll find a myriad bugs
>   That stink and crawl and bite;
> If doubtful of the truth of this,
>   Get up and strike a light.

It must have been the poet's up-bringing or his being overpowered by other ills that prevented him from finishing the work so well begun. Let me endeavour to complete the picture –

> Within, without, vile odours dense
>   Assail the unwary nose;
> Behind, the grunter squeaks and squeals
>   And baffles all repose;
> Add clouds of tiny, buzzing things,
>   Mosquitoes – if you please;
> And if the sum is not enough,
>   Why, bless me, there are fleas.

7) *Rats an article of food*
(J.H. Gray, *China*, II, p. 77)
The flesh of rats is also an article of food. In a street at Canton, named Hing-loong Kai, where there are many poulterers' shops, rats are exposed for sale with ducks, geese, and fowls. They are salted and dried, and eaten by both men and women. The women, however, who eat the flesh of these animals are generally those who are becoming bald, it being considered by the Chinese as a hair restorative. In the winter, when rats are in season, the windows of the poulterers' shops in the street which I have named are often crowded with dried rats. The consumption of such food is by no means universal, but the practice of eating rats prevails to some extent in different parts of the empire.

8) *Chinese food*
(A. Colquhoun, *Across Chrysê*, I, pp. 77–9)
Accustomed as I have been to rougher modes of travel, and infinitely worse fare in other lands, notably in Burmah, our life on the river was comparatively one of luxury; but our cuisine would, I fear, hardly

recommend itself to fastidious Western palates. Pork in various forms was naturally a favourite with our Chinese *chef*; 'an he could he would' have served nothing else.

But as stewed pork, roast pork, pork sausages (terrible things they are!) and pig's-foot *gelée* are apt to pall upon the uncultivated Western palate, we were forced to enter a protest against the too frequent repetition of these Chinese dainties. . . . We had a hard struggle with the cook, but he relaxed so far as to vary the pork *menu* with dried duck and salt eggs. He, however, spared us that favourite *morceau* with the Chinese, the pi-tan, or sulphurated eggs. Shark's fin and bird's-nest were, of course, rare dainties, not for us.

However, to be serious, Chinese food is by no means the horrible mess which Europeans generally believe it to be. Its bad reputation has not been altogether justly earned. The ideas that people at home have on this subject are equalled only by the other absurd notions entertained in regard to the Chinese. The fixed impression in England is that puppy-dog, cat and rat, and so on, form articles of the daily *menu*. This, of course, is utterly absurd.

A few of the very poorest class in Canton do eat them, it is true. The food of a poor family is usually rice, with a bowl of soup to wash it down; something salt and tasty as a condiment; pork, vegetables and macaroni, – curry being unknown! With the wealthier the fare is rich soup, oyster or shell-fish; pork (stewed or otherwise), fish, boiled fowl, roast duck and vegetables. With the poorest people, rice and salt cabbage or salt fish, with a *suspicion* of pork only, is the daily ration. Our boatmen ['s food] . . . often looked by no means bad; eleven hours' work would make me relish it, I am sure; – though I confess that a trial did not prepossess me in its favour!

9) *Chinese traders on the middle Amur*
(T.W. Atkinson, *Travels in the Region of the Upper and Lower Amoor*, p. 474)
The Chinese trader penetrates to every inhabited spot, with tea and various articles of clothing, but the greatest portion of his cargo is brandy, and he here, as elsewhere, soon strips the people of their valuable skins for one-tenth part of their value, paid in this most disagreeable composition. His customers are then compelled to make over to him a portion of the next year's produce to procure the few

necessaries they require, which are only to be obtained at an enormous price. These scoundrels become rich by the demoralisation and ruin they produce.

10) *Discovery of the written language of the Lolo*
(E.C. Baber, *Travels and Researches in Western China*, pp. 125–6)
After a hasty dinner I summoned my native clerk and we began an exhaustive exploration of thousands of documents. The search was not so difficult as might appear, since the printed papers ... formed three-fourths of the mass. ... The Lolos do not possess the art of printing, and we had therefore only to examine the written documents. These were principally drafts of letters, rough accounts, and children's copy-books, the latter in great number. Not wishing our unhandsome inquisitiveness to be made public, we had frequently to relax operations on account of interruptions, so that we did not complete our work until soon after midnight. We found nothing to our purpose in any of the packages; but under the last few, almost in the furthest corner, we discerned with gloating eyes the scrap of writing of which a facsimile is appended – a specimen of Lolo characters with the sound of each word, or syllable, approximately indicated in Chinese.

It might have been expected that the Lolo writing would turn out to be some form of Pali. It shows, however, no relation to that system, but seems to take after the Chinese method. In any case the discovery possesses no small value and raises so many interesting questions that a little exultation may be pardoned. A new people may be discovered anywhere, a new language any day; but a new system of writing is a find of exceeding rarity. Many a rival galled the kibes of Columbus, but the achievement of Cadmus has been deemed so astonishing that his very existence is now denied!

11) *Non-Chinese races of Western and South-Western China*
(A. Hosie, *Three Years in Western China*, pp. 225–7)
Our knowledge of these races is defective, for the simple reason that no foreigner has ever paid them a lengthened visit. ... Nor is this a matter for surprise, as the opportunities, which foreigners possess of visiting these tribes, whose haunts are removed from beaten tracks, are few and far between; and those few who have had such opportunities have been too much occupied with other work to study ethnological

details or acquire a new language. [. . .]

In what does the traveller's day usually consist? He gets up at daybreak, hurries on to the end of the stage, writes up an account of the day's journey, endeavours to get something to eat, and tries to enjoy a few hours' sleep ere the labours of another day begin. The miseries of travel, too, breed a feeling of restlessness. . . . But all the comfort the traveller in these regions may expect, and too frequently gets, is shelter in a miserable mud hovel without chair or table – hardly a promising spot in which to commence ethnological studies.

Nor is this all; given a chair and a table, the next difficulty is to find the man whose characteristics it is intended to study. The treatment which these aborigines receive at the hands of the Chinese, and the contempt in which they are held by them, have induced a timidity which is hard to overcome, and they have often expressed to me their fears that they would get into trouble through accepting my invitation to visit me.

In traversing the country between the Ta-tu River in Western Ssŭ-ch'uan and the north-west frontier of Yün-nan, I have frequently seen so-called Man-tzŭ suddenly quit the roadway and conceal themselves in the bordering brushwood and tall reeds until we had passed. And even when an interview has with difficulty been obtained, my visitors were always anxious to get away as soon as possible, so that the most the traveller can do is to note down a few of their more common words, without attempting the analysis of even a few simple sentences.

A few short vocabularies are all that I was able to collect during my journeys; but, towards the end of 1884, chance threw in my way an opportunity of entering more fully into the language of the principal branch of the aborigines of Kuei-chow, known to the Chinese as the Hei or Black Miao, or, as they call themselves, the Phö. [. . .]

I should state that, according to my teacher, there is no written character, and my aim was to preserve a specimen of a tongue which must sooner or later become extinct. Of late years, the authorities of the province of Kuei-chow have been endeavouring to compel the Miao-tzŭ to adopt the Chinese dress and learn the Chinese language. Their efforts, too, are meeting with considerable success, and it is safe to predict that the Phö tongue is within a measurable distance of extinction.

12) *A Great Soldier*
(T.T. Cooper, *Travels of a Pioneer of Commerce*, pp. 146–7)

About a mile from the city I alighted for a walk, and just before entering the gates happened to take off my spectacles to wipe them, when a little girl exclaimed, 'Yang-jen! Yang-jen!' This immediately attracted the attention of a number of soldiers and youthful candidates for military honours, who were returning from the annual competition in archery. They at once surrounded me, hooting loudly; one fellow, evidently the worse for samshu, caught hold of my skirts and nearly pulled me backwards; the usual crowd speedily assembled, and things began to look awkward. A happy thought occurred to me, viz., to chance an appeal to the sense of the ridiculous, which is strongly developed in John Chinaman; so I made my persecutor a reverential bow, and, striking an attitude, exclaimed, with a wink to the bystanders, 'Surely this is a great soldier!'

Now, he was hump-backed, and very ugly, and by no means heroical, and the crowd yelled with derisive laughter. The hero, much abashed, let go my dress at once, and in retreating tumbled down, whereupon I jumped over him and got away. My coolies arrived on the instant, and took me into my chair, congratulating me with boisterous laughter on my escape from 'the great soldier'.

Nothing is easier than to influence a Chinese crowd, if collected by curiosity only. They are fond of a joke, and are always readier to laugh than to come to blows.

I had now practised self-restraint among the Celestials for so long, that I did not on this occasion betray the slightest symptom of anger. Had I done so, the crowd would have caught the infection, and vented their wrath on me. As it was, I took it all as a joke, and made them laugh in spite of themselves, and so escaped further molestation. On such trifles may the life of a traveller in China hang, for this crowd, easily moved to laughter, would have been as easily led on to bloodshed.

13) *The Loo-din-chow suspension bridge*
(T.T. Cooper, *Travels of a Pioneer of Commerce*, pp. 197–8)

Its construction is very faulty. Nine large chains, not quite so thick as a ship's cable, with a space of four feet between each, are stretched over large square buttresses built against each bank, and securely built into masses of masonry; the roadway is simply a flooring of boards, unsecured by any ballast or handrail; and the vibration is so great, that at times it is almost impossible to keep one's feet. At noon every day the gates leading to the bridge are closed until 4 p.m., and no person is allowed to cross, as the terrific winds sweeping along the gorge between the mountains which rise on either bank render the passage excessively dangerous. For a year or two after its construction it is said to have answered its purpose very well; but of late years most shocking accidents, causing great loss of life, have occurred through the chains breaking.

CULTURE

At the beginning of the nineteenth century, western knowledge and appreciation of Chinese culture other than of the applied arts was limited. Du Halde had commented cautiously that to understand well what the excellence of Chinese poetry consisted of, it was necessary to be skilled in the language. One of the first to claim that degree of skill was John Francis Davis. He compared Chinese poetic technique with that of the classical poets, and with Hebrew and French examples, and sought to explain why Chinese poetry had not found admirers in the west (1).

As western knowledge of China increased, a scholarly industry was established which provided a broader appreciation of aspects of China's cultural achievement. An early example was the publication of the *Chinese Repository*, which appeared monthly between 1832 and 1851, the object of which was to diffuse correct information concerning China. On the China coast, and among China-watchers and academics in the West, societies were formed to pool information. By 1871 the North China Branch of the Royal Asiatic Society, which had begun in 1857 as the Shanghai Literary and Scientific Society, had its own buildings, library and a museum. Another impetus to Chinese studies was the endowment of academic chairs at universities, an early example being the Chair of Chinese at King's College, London, first occupied by Samuel Fearon in 1847.

These activities did little to increase the appreciation of Chinese culture. It was not surprising that language students should express their frustration and call for a cultural imperialism to reduce Chinese to an Indo-European model (2). The translation of Chinese raised problems and caused scholarly disputes (3). Even by the middle of the century few westerners had acquired a sufficient knowledge of Chinese literature to venture a judgement of its quality (4). But by 1874 the study of Chinese literature had become sufficiently common for the publication, by W.F. Mayers, of *The Chinese Reader's Manual*, a handbook of literary reference (5). Nevertheless R.K. Douglas, the Professor of Chinese at King's College, London, could still argue that Chinese literature had little to offer the western reader (6).

Usually the attitude towards other aspects of Chinese culture was condescending and dismissive. S. Wells Williams wrote at some length about Chinese musical notation, musical instruments, etc., but showed little appreciation of what he had heard (7). T.T. Cooper was rather more impressed by the Szechuanese musicians who performed for him (8). Throughout the nineteenth century, Chinese painting was little appreciated, unless it was done in the western style (9). In 1856, Owen Jones had scarcely a positive remark to make about Chinese ornament (10). Even by the end of the century western knowledge of Chinese pictorial art was slight (11).

In the eighteenth century Chinese architecture and landscape gardening had been the inspiration of rococo and chinoiserie. A century later, much of that appeal had dissipated. One of the few buildings mentioned with favour was the Porcelain Tower, the fifteenth-century pagoda outside the walls of Nanking. MM. Callery and Yvan inspected it shortly before it was destroyed by the Taipings in 1856 (12). The other example of architecture praised extravagantly by westerners was the Summer Palace. But the true value they placed on it was revealed in 1860 when it was looted and burned by British and French troops (13 and 14). A different view of Chinese architecture was revealed in the amusing, condescending, anecdote told by Colonel Fisher (15). Dr W.A.P. Martin, describing the Hanlin Academy, the so-called All Souls' College of China, gave a different explanation of Chinese limitations in matters of architecture (16).

1) *The test of the poetry of China*
(J.F. Davis, *Poeseos Sinensis Commentarii*, pp. 39–41)
Unless submitted with some degree of allowance to the touchstone of European taste, the poetry of China might possibly succeed but indifferently. The test, if it be not considerately applied, is not only an illiberal, but an absurd one; and we have no right hastily to condemn the devotion which the ultra-Gangetic muse ... inspires in her own native haunts; or to be surprised at the number of her exalted admirers, from Confucius down to Keënlong, – considering that

national taste is the most conventional and capricious thing in the world . . . and that even with the same old copies to refer to, and with a general similarity of institutions and customs, the different nations of the great European community vary, on such points, not a little among themselves. [. . .]

There seem to be two causes, to which Chinese literature, of the lighter or ornamental kind, has owed its indifferent reception in the West – first, a want of choice and selection in the subjects – and secondly, a considerable absence of taste and judgment in the mode of treating them. It is really too much to expect that people will trouble themselves to look at what is either stupid and good-for-nothing in itself, or so marred in the intermediate process, as to have lost all the attraction that it possessed in the original state. Let us only place the Chinese in our own situation on such occasions, and imagine the dismay of some fastidious scholar who should unluckily stumble upon one of our street-ballads, *done* into bad Chinese, that is, with a verbal adherence to the original. It would either prove a perfect enigma, which is supposing the most fortunate case, – or he would thank his stars that the broad ocean divided him from such savages. . . . The interests and reputation of Chinese literature in Europe therefore seem to demand, that its professors take some pains to render its introduction as attractive as possible, by a careful selection of the best subjects, and by treating these in such a manner as shall interest the greatest number of tasteful and cultivated readers. To weary the attention with a mere list of barbariphonous and uncouth names, to produce some bald and miserably verbal translation . . . is in fact scaring away attention from a new subject, which, with a little discretion, might be rendered sufficiently attractive even to *general* readers.

2) *Deficiencies of the Chinese Language*
(W.H. Medhurst, *China*, pp. 167–8)
In the science of grammar, the Chinese have made no progress; and among the host of their literati, no one seems to have turned his attention to this subject. They have not learned to distinguish the parts of speech or to define and designate case, gender, number, person, mood, or tense; they neither decline their nouns, nor conjugate their verbs, while regimen and concord are with them based on no written

rules. Not that the language is incapable of expressing these ideas, or that a scheme of grammar could not be drawn up for the Chinese tongue; but the natives themselves have no notion of such distinctions, and could hardly be made to comprehend them. They have treatises on the art of speaking and writing, but these handle the subject in a manner peculiar to themselves. They divide their words into 'living and dead', 'real and empty'; a 'living word' is a verb, and 'a dead word' a substantive; while both of these are called 'real', in distinction from particles, which are termed 'empty'. They also distinguish words into 'important' and 'unimportant'. The chief aim of Chinese writers is to dispose the particles aright, and he who can do this is denominated a clever scholar.

3) *On the translation of Chinese proper names*
(T.T. Meadows, *The Chinese and Their Rebellions*, p. 62)
... M. Huc says that the officer with whom he was lodged '*se nommait Pao ngan ou Trésor cachée*'. – In these two words he violates grammar in a way that I should not pardon in a sinologue of three months' standing. In Chinese the adjective invariably precedes the noun, and here the two Chinese words, if held to be in grammatical connexion at all, must be rendered 'precious or valuable secret'. But I object altogether to M. Huc's translating of this and many other proper names; which the Chinese regard only as such. Such translating is often very forced; and though it is amusing – very oriental, and ten-thousand-miles-offy I admit – still it is so at the certain cost of propagating misconception, by increasing that grotesque colouring already too much the light in which Occidentals are habituated to see the Chinese. . . . A Frenchman would not be considered to have rendered the views of his countrymen on 'British eccentricity' more truthful, who, on returning from a visit to England, would say that he had landed at Mare-de-foié, Chasseur de colombe ou Plier-bouche instead of Liverpool, Dover or Plymouth; and that he had travelled from the latter port to London by way of Bain, Lecture et Virginité, instead of Bath, Reading and Maidenhead.

4) *Chinese literature*
(S. Wells Williams, *The Middle Kingdom*, I, pp. 718–19)
Such is the general range and survey of Chinese literature, according to the Catalogue of the Imperial Libraries. It is, take it in a mass, a

stupendous monument of human toil, fitly compared, so far as it is calculated to instruct its readers in useful knowledge, to their Great Wall, which can neither protect from its enemies, nor be of any real use to its makers. Its deficiencies are glaring. No treatises on the geography of foreign countries nor truthful narratives of travels abroad are contained in it, nor any account of the languages of their inhabitants, their history, or their governments. Philological works in other languages than those spoken within the Empire are unknown, and must, owing to the nature of the language, remain so until foreigners prepare them. Works on natural history, medicine, and philology are few and useless, while those on mathematics and the exact sciences are much less popular and useful than they might be; and in the great range of theology, founded on the true basis of the Bible, there is almost nothing. The character of the people has been mostly formed by their ancient books, and this correlate influence has tended to repress independent investigation in the pursuit of truth, though not to destroy it. A new infusion of science, religion, and descriptive geography and history will lead to comparison with other countries, and bring out whatever in it is good.

5) *A canon of Chinese literary art*
(W.F. Mayers, *The Chinese Reader's Manual*, p. iii)
The wealth of illustration furnished to a Chinese writer by the records of his long-descended past is a feature which must be remarked at even the most elementary stage of acquaintance with the literature of the country. In every branch of composition, ingenious parallels and the introduction of borrowed phrases, considered elegant in proportion to their concise and recondite character, enjoy in Chinese style the same place of distinction that is accorded in European literature to originality of thought or novelty of diction. The Chinese are not, indeed, singular in the taste for metaphor or quotation adopted from the events or from the masterpieces of expression in the past. No European writer – it is needless to observe – can dispense with illustrations drawn from a multitude of earlier sources, and in even the most familiar language fragments of history and legend lie embedded, almost unperceived. What with ourselves, however, is at the most an exceptional feature, takes with the Chinese the character of a canon of literary art. Intricacies of allusion and quotation present themselves,

consequently, at every turn in the written language, to furnish a clue to some of which, and at the same time to bring together from various sources an epitome of historical and biographical details much needed by every student, have been the principal objects of the present work.

6) *On the defects of Chinese literature*
(R.K. Douglas, *The Language and Literature of China*, pp. 116–18)
This play furnishes us with a very good type of Chinese plays in general. The incidents are true to life, but they have no psychological interest about them. There is no delineation of character in it, and there is nothing in the plot to make it more appropriate for the groundwork of a play than for that of a novel. In the works of fiction we are treated only to the same crude narration of facts, without any just representation of nature. Exaggerated sentiments ... fill the pages of their works of fiction, rendering them favourites only with those who are taught to judge of them according to their own standard of taste. Of the characters portrayed, we have to judge only from actions attributed to them, which are strung together with no connecting links, except those supplied by the iteration of details, which are wearisome to a degree. Several novels have been translated into English by Sir John Davis and others; but, from the causes I have described, few have attracted any public interest. Some of their shorter tales, being to a great extent purged of the cumbrous repetitions common to larger works, are better capable of translation, and the novelty of many of the situations and incidents serves to keep alive the attention of the reader. Unfortunately the tone of most Chinese novels is not such as to afford any palliation for the dreariness of their contents ...

If then, having considered the past and present literature of China, we cast a glance into the future, the prospect is not encouraging. Already every subject within the scope of Chinese authors has been largely treated of and infinitely elaborated. Every grain of wheat has long ago been beaten out of it, and any further labour expended upon it can but be only as thrashing out straw. The only hope for the future of the literature is that afforded by the importation of foreign knowledge and experience into the country. For many years these can only be introduced in the shape of translations of books. But the time will come when Chinese authors will think for themselves; and when that period arrives, they will learn to estimate their present loudly-vaunted literature at its true value.

7) *Chinese music*
(S. Wells Williams, *The Middle Kingdom*, II, pp. 93–4)

The utility of music in encouraging the soldiers and exciting them to the charge is fully appreciated, but to our notions it no more deserves the name of music than the collection of half-drilled louts in petticoats does that of an army, when compared with a European force. Still, its antiquity, if nothing else, renders it a subject of great interest to the musical student, while its power over the people seems to be none the less because it is unscientific. However small their attainments in the theory and practice of music, no nation gives to this art a higher place. It was regarded by Confucius as an essential part in the government of a state. . . . It is remarked of the sage himself that having heard a tune in one of his ramblings, he did not know the taste of food for three weeks after – but, with all deference to the feelings of so distinguished a man, we cannot help thinking his food might have been quite as palatable without music, if it was no better then than it is at the present day.

8) *Szechwanese musicians*
(T.T. Cooper, *Travels of a Pioneer of Commerce*, pp. 162–3)

Our musicians were supposed to be the first artists in Chen-tu; and for six long hours they kept my guests and Philip in raptures. One of the performers was blind, and played a stringed instrument which gave forth really very sweet music. It was a species of dulcimer, shaped like a toy harmonicon, but, in the place of glass, there were sets of wire strings, like those of a piano, upon which the performer played with two small wooden hammers, covered with leather. Another played on a three-stringed fiddle; and a third on the bones; while they sang in turn in different voices, – one singing bass, another tenor, and the third soprano.

They carried with them a case of small books, each containing the words of an opera, which, before commencing, they handed to us, and my military friend selected several favourite pieces, which were played during the evening. The Chinese play entirely by ear; and although, according to European ideas, they know nothing of music, yet, after their own fashion, they are no mean performers.

9) *The Sir Thomas Lawrence of China*
(H.C. Sirr, *China and the Chinese*, I, pp. 107–8)

Lum-qua is called by Europeans the Sir Thomas Lawrence of China, and he well deserves this proud distinction, as the colouring of this artist's oil-paintings is exceedingly fine: although his ideas of female beauty differ materially from our own: in the course of conversation we asked his opinion of an English belle then at Canton, and the reply was completely characteristic of a Chinaman's ideas of female beauty; her face is too round, she has colour in her cheeks, her eyes are too blue, too large; she's too tall, too plump . . . *and she has feet so large that she can walk upon them.* In Lum-qua's atélier we saw many portraits both of Europeans and Chinese, many of which were excellent likenesses, and although deficient in light and shade, were executed in a most masterly manner; but the great defect in Lum-qua's portraits is a deficiency of life and expression: our attention was particularly attracted by what we considered a very pretty female face, of round plump contour, the eyes possibly rather too small, the painting representing a Chinese lady: we asked the artist who the lady was, when he replied, 'that nobody, that fancy portrait for Englishman, that not Chinaman beauty, that China beauty'; pointing to the portrait of a boat-woman, which most assuredly ill accorded with our ideas of female loveliness, as the face was expressionless, lean, colourless, and sallow.

10) *Chinese ornament*
(O. Jones, *The Grammar of Ornament*, introduction to chapter XIV)

Notwithstanding the high antiquity of the civilisation of the Chinese, and the perfection which all their manufacturing processes reached ages before our time, they do not appear to have made much advance in the Fine Arts . . .

In their ornamentation, with which the world is so familiar through the numerous manufactured articles of every kind which have been imported into this country, they do not appear to have gone beyond that point which is reached by every people in an early stage of civilisation. . . . In the conception of pure form they are even behind the New Zealander; but they possess, in common with all Eastern nations, the happy instinct of harmonising colours. As this is more a faculty than an acquirement, it is just what we should expect; the arriving at an appreciation of pure form is a more subtle process, and is the result of either more highly endowed natural instincts, or of the development of primitive ideas, by successive generations of artists improving on each other's efforts.

The general forms of many of the Chinese porcelain vases are remarkable for the beauty of their outline, but not more so than the rude water-bottles of porous clay which the untutored Arabian potter fashions daily on the banks of the Nile, assisted only by the instincts of his gentle race; and the pure form of the Chinese vases is often destroyed by the addition of grotesque or other unmeaning ornaments, built up upon the surface, not growing from it: from which we argue, that they can possess an appreciation of form, but in a minor degree. [. . .]

On the whole, Chinese ornament is a very faithful expression of the nature of this peculiar people; its characteristic feature is oddness, – we cannot call it capricious, for caprice is the playful wandering of a lively imagination; but the Chinese are totally unimaginative, and all their works are accordingly wanting in the highest grace of art, – the ideal.

11) *Chinese pictorial art*
(H.A. Giles, *An Introduction to the History of Chinese Pictorial Art*, preface to the first edition)
This is the first attempt which has been made so far, in any European language, to deal even cursorily, with the history of Chinese pictorial art. The Chinese themselves have produced scores of volumes on the history and practice of painting, but there has been little, if any, direct appeal to these works – certainly nothing in the way of translation – on the part of the few foreigners who have written, all too briefly, on the subject.

12) *The Porcelain Tower of Nanking*
(MM. Callery and Yvan, *History of the Insurrection*, pp. 234–5)
The tower of Nankin is the magnificent complement of the pagoda Pao-Ngan-Se. It is of an octagonal form, and not less than seventy metres in height. At a distance it appears entirely white, but on approaching it we can discern the variety of colors and gilding with which it is covered. A large pedestal of rough hewn marble is the base of the monument, round which it forms a broad landing-place, which

is reached by some ten steps. The large hall, which serves as the ground floor to the temple, is about a dozen or fifteen metres in depth, and about eight metres in height. Above this hall rise successively nine floors, each seven metres high, and separated from each other by a series of roofs or cornices, which project to the extent of a metre, and form those angles curved upwards, which characterize Chinese architecture. An incommodious staircase inside the edifice leads to its summit, and on every floor is a room of less diameter than that below it. The bulk of the monument is of common brick, and its thickness is four metres at the base, and two and a half at the summit. The outside of the walls is covered over with plates of common white porcelain, joined perfectly together. In the lower floors the porcelain is merely adorned by a few stamped ornaments, of no great depth; but in the upper floors are seen a number of niches, in which are placed statuettes and idols, apparently gilded. In the middle of the hall on each floor is an altar, dedicated to Buddha. The spire which surmounts the tower is ten metres high. It is composed of a strong stem, round which a broad spiral piece of iron is twisted, and terminates in a large ball, which is said to be of solid gold. The height and peculiar brightness of this tower cause Nankin to be recognized at a great distance; and it has served as a beacon to the first English and French ships-of-war that ascended the Yang-Tze-Kiang.

13) *The Summer Palace before its destruction*
(R.J.L. M'Ghee, *How We Got to Pekin*, pp. 211–12)
The grounds extended for six or seven miles in every direction, and further towards the hills. If you can, you must imagine a vast labyrinth of picturesque rocks and noble timber, lakes and streams, summer-houses roofed with porcelain of the imperial yellow, theatres and their store-houses, filled with all the paraphernalia for masquerades upon a gigantic scale, one theatre and its belongings covering from five to ten acres of ground, all richly planted around; temples more numerous still, full of quaint deities (some of them, as it has since turned out, of gold), and every building . . . filled with works of Chinese art of great age, beauty, and value, and in the background a range of hills, their outline cut clear against the sky; you must think of all the best gifts of nature . . . then deck the scene with all the world-famed skill of the Celestial in landscape gardening, thrown in here and there so well that

it looks like nature's own hand; scatter those beautiful buildings round, with their gorgeous roofs peeping through the dark forest timber; see, there is an imperial stag bounding across your paths; conjure up the quaint old Chinese bridge here and there, to carry you across the feeder of some placid lake, with its ornamental waterfowl: and you may be able to form some very faint and indistinct idea of the Ewen-ming-Ewen . . .

14) *The burning of the Summer Palace, October, 1860*
(R. Swinhoe, *Narrative of the North China Campaign*, pp. 329–31)
The First Division, under General Michel, was detailed for this work of destruction, and betimes on the 18th started for the Palace, where the buildings were apportioned to the different companies to destroy. The French refused to co-operate, as they condemned the measure as a piece of barbarism, forgetting that the chief mischief had been committed by themselves, not only in purloining and demolishing everything that the Palace contained in the way of art, but also in having permitted their men to incendiarise the choicest rooms of the Emperor.

Ere long a dense column of smoke rising to the sky indicated that the work had commenced, and as the day waned the column increased in magnitude, and grew denser and denser, wafting in the shape of a large cloud over Pekin, and having the semblance of a fearful thunderstorm impending. As we approached the Palace the crackling and rushing noise of fire was appalling, and the sun shining through the masses of smoke gave a sickly hue to every plant and tree, and the red flame gleaming on the faces of the troops engaged made them appear like demons glorying in the destruction of what they could not replace. The night was a warm one, and as roof after roof crashed in, smothering the fire that devoured its sustaining walls, and belching out instead large volumes of smoke, it betokened to our minds a sad portent of the fate of this antique empire, its very entrails being consumed by internecine war, how it has compelled those nations that might have been its prop to aid in its destruction, and how, beset on all sides, with nought to turn to for succour, it at last succumbs with a burst of vapour, lost in the ashes of its former self.

15) *A model barrack*
(Lt.-Col. Fisher, *Personal Narrative of Three Years' Service in China*, pp. 70–1)

He gave an amusing instance of the imitative genius of his nation on one occasion. It was determined to build some wooden huts on the heights, and Sing-chong agreed to execute the work. He was given a sheet of paper, having on it at the bottom, a *plan* of the building, showing the joists and flooring, above that an *elevation*, showing the boarded sides and windows, and above that again a cross *section*, showing the proportions of the gable as well as the sides of the hut. After it had all been explained to him in pigeon English, he was told to make a rough sort of model, according as he understood it, before preparing the material for the actual work. In a couple of days the model was presented. It was a pagoda-looking affair of the following construction. The lower story was square, each side being the length of what the building should be; it was framed and boarded, and was, in fact, the *plan* of the building turned up on edge, forming the four sides of the figure; above this was a story, also square, with windows, which was the *elevation*; and the whole having been covered with a flat roof, he put in the centre a square pagoda with a pyramidal roof, each side with the width of the cross *section* of the hut. He hinted that we had forgotten the doors and staircases, and that he had taken the liberty to add a railing round the edge of the flat roof, to prevent the soldiers falling off when they walked forth out of the top pagoda.

16) *Reflections on the Hanlin Yuan or Imperial Academy*
(W.A.P. Martin, *The Chinese*, pp. 6–7)
But things in China are not to be estimated by ordinary rules. Here the decay of a building is no indication of the decadence of the institution which it represents. The public buildings of the Chinese are, for the most part, mean and contemptible in comparison with those of Western nations; but it would not be less erroneous for us to judge their civilization by the state of their architecture than for them, as they are prone to do, to measure ours by the tape-line of our tailor. With them architecture is not a fine art; public edifices of every class are constructed on a uniform model; and even in private dwellings there is no such thing as novelty or variety of design. The original idea of both is incapable of much development; the wooden frame and limited height giving them an air of meanness; while the windowless wall . . . diminishes, if it does not destroy, the desire for aesthetic effect. Materialistic as the people are in their habits of thought, their

government, based on ancient maxims, has sought to repress rather than encourage the tendency to luxury in this direction. The genius of China does not affect excellence in material arts. With more propriety than ancient Rome she might apply to herself the lines of the Roman poet:

> *'Excudent alii spirantia mollius aera*
> *. . . regere imperio populos . . .*
> *Hae tibi erunt artes; pacisque imponere morem.'*

For not only is the Chinese notoriously backward in all those accomplishments in which the Roman excelled, but, without being warlike, he has equalled the Roman in the extent of his conquests, and surpassed him in the permanence of his possessions. With him the art of government is the 'great study'; and all else – science, literature, religion – merely subsidiary.

ON THE CHARACTER OF
THE CHINESE

Until the Opium War, the small western community living at Canton and Macao produced most of the new writing on China. One vehicle for its publication was the *Chinese Repository*, edited by two American missionaries, E.C. Bridgman and S. Wells Williams. It was an indication of the restricted knowledge of China at that time that 'Philosinensis' (the Revd C. Gutzlaff) described China as a nation characterized by its sameness (1), and that another contributor repeated the stereotype of the Chinese, that they were 'our antipodes in many things besides geographical ambition' (2).

These views were not typical of the nineteenth century, which saw an increasing sharpness and condescension in western estimates of Chinese character. The Treaty of Nanking, 1842, imposed the first 'unequal treaty' on China. Palmerston spelled out the new tone to be adopted by British officials towards the Chinese (3), and Rutherford Alcock, the British Consul at Shanghai asserted the importance of coercing the Chinese into paying due respect to the British and into allowing foreigners wider access (4).

With this wider access came a great increase in the number of books which offered assessments of the Chinese character. One of the most influential of these was S. Wells Williams's *The Middle Kingdom*, first published in 1847. Williams rejected the 'contrariety' view and suggested that China should be called the 'Middle Kingdom' 'from the Chinese holding a middle place between civilization and barbarism' (5). The Revd William Gillespie repeated the eighteenth-century stereotype of changeless China, but gave it an additional twist with a reference to progress in the West (6). George Wingrove Cooke, *The Times'* special correspondent, claimed to have resisted the temptation to write an essay on the subject, but his book was full of sweeping and unflattering assertions about the Chinese (7).

One of the commonest generalizations applied to the Chinese was that they were cruel and indifferent to pain. Western medical men felt qualified to comment on this issue. Dr Toogood Downing observed operations being performed in Canton in the 1820s and speculated on the fortitude of Chinese patients (8). Nearly forty years later, Dr Gordon, after having spent two years in China with the allied forces, offered his opinion on the same subject (9).

Not all estimates of the 'Chinese character' were unfavourable. D.F. Rennie, the surgeon to the legation guards in Peking, felt obliged to counter what to him were unfair aspersions (10). A more positive assessment was made by W.A.P. Martin, who, in 1868, declared that a 'mental awakening' was taking place, by which 'the Chinese mind will be brought proportionally nearer to our own'. The agency of this change was 'Christian enterprise' (11).

The debate on the Chinese character continued through the century. In 1872, W.H. Medhurst, the British Consul at Shanghai, contrasted two 'vague' and 'erroneous' views of China and the Chinese (12). In *The Foreigner in Far Cathay* he attempted to prove that 'with a few drawbacks of character they exhibit many interesting and even commendable traits'. Archdeacon Gray prevaricated – he found it difficult to speak justly on their moral character (13), but Samuel Wells Williams, in the revised edition of *The Middle Kingdom*, asserted confidently that a missionary was better able to ascertain the 'falsity of the Chinese' than were either ambassadors or merchants, who had both purveyed a misleading view of this aspect of the Chinese character (14).

The attempt to define the Chinese character reached its height in Arthur Smith's *Chinese Characteristics*. Smith, also an American missionary, referred modestly to his qualifications to write a book on such a topic:

The circumstance that a person has lived for twenty-two years in China is no more a guarantee that he is competent to write of the characteristics of the Chinese, than the fact that another man has for twenty-two years been buried in a silver mine is proof that he is a fit person to compose a treatise on metallurgy . . .[1]

Nevertheless, fortified by the approving opinions of a number of other foreign residents of even greater seniority than himself, Smith did offer his views. One of the topics he discussed was Chinese benevolence, of which he was sceptical (15). His observations on this subject were later challenged by the traveller Isabella Bird (16).

1) *The sameness to be found in China*
('Philosinensis', 'Remarks on the history and chronology of China', p. 74)
It is a trite remark, that in no country of Europe, or of the whole globe, is there so much sameness to be found as in China. Observe the physiognomy, the character, and the institutions of the people, and you find only a slight difference between the inhabitants of the several provinces. View their cities, houses, temples, and public courts, and how little do they differ from each other, though separated in distance more than a thousand miles. The diversities in the Chinese dress, and in their whole mode of life, are indeed so slight as to be almost imperceptible to a stranger, who, on seeing them for the first time, can scarcely distinguish an inhabitant of Peking from a native of Canton. This uniformity pervades also their whole literature; the Chinese thoughts are *stereotyped* in their classics, and the learned individual or author merely gives a new edition.

2) *The Chinese our antipodes*
('Illustrations of men and things in China', pp. 106–7)
As I had come to the country to reside for sometime, I made inquiries respecting a teacher, and ... [found] one who happily understood English. On entering the room, he stood at the door, and instead of coming forward and shaking my hands, he politely bowed, and shook his own before his breast. I looked upon this custom as a decided improvement upon our mode, especially in doubtful cases; and requested him to be seated. I knew I was about to study a language without an alphabet, but was somewhat astonished to find him begin at what I had all my life previously considered the end of the book. He read the date of the publication, 'The fifth year, tenth month, and first day.' 'We arrange our dates differently,' I observed, and begged him to begin to read, which he did from the top to the bottom, then proceeding from the right to the left ... [...]

On going abroad, I met so many things contrary to all my preconceived ideas of propriety, that I readily assented to a friend's observation 'that the Chinese were our antipodes in many things besides geography'. 'Indeed,' said I, 'it is so; I shall almost expect shortly to see a man walking on his head; look, there's a woman in trowsers, and a party of gentlemen in petticoats; she is smoking a segar, and they are fanning themselves'; [however] . . . on passing them, I saw the latter wore tight undergarments. We soon after met the comprador of the house dressed in a complete suit of white, and I stopped and asked him what merry-making he was invited to; with a look of the deepest concern, he said he was just returning from burying his father.

3) *Palmerston's view of the tone to be adopted in China*
(Lord Palmerston to Sir John Davis, 3 October 1846, quoted in H.B. Morse, *The International Relations of the Chinese Empire*, I, p. 385)
We shall lose all the vantage ground we have gained by our victories in China, if we take a low tone. We must take especial care not to descend from the relative position which we have acquired. If we maintain that position morally, by the tone of our intercourse, we shall not be obliged to recover it by forcible acts; but if we permit the Chinese . . . to resume . . . their former tone of affected superiority, we shall very soon be compelled to come to blows with them again. Of course we ought . . . to abstain from giving the Chinese any ground of complaint, and much more from anything like provocation or affront; but we must stop on the very threshold any attempt on their part to treat us otherwise than as their equals, and we must make them all clearly understand, though in the civilest terms, that our treaty rights must be respected. The Chinese must learn and be convinced, that if they attack our people and our factories, they will be shot; and if they ill-treat innocent Englishmen, who are quietly exercising their treaty right of walking about the streets of Canton, they will be punished. . . . Depend upon it that the best way of keeping any men quiet, is to let them see that you are able and determined to repel force by force; and the Chinese are not in the least different, in this respect, from the rest of mankind.

4) *The respect due to a British subject*
(R. Alcock, 'Note on our present position and the state of our relations

---

with China', 19 January 1849, in A. Michie, *The Englishman in China*, I, p. 424)
A salutary dread of the immediate consequences of violence offered to British subjects, the certainty of its creating greater trouble and danger to the native authorities personally than even the most vigorous efforts to protect the foreigner and seize their assailants will entail, seems to be the best and only protection in this country for Englishmen. When the Chinese authorities of all ranks, from the viceroy at Nanking to the lowest police runners, are thoroughly imbued with this feeling, it will not only rouse them to greater energy but find its way to the populace by certain steps, and render such exertion unnecessary, and the nationality of an Englishman will become his safeguard.

5) *The most civilized pagan nation*
(S. Wells Williams, *The Middle Kingdom*, preface to the first edition, pp. xiv–xv)
Another object aimed at, has been to divest the Chinese people and civilization of that peculiar and almost undefinable impression of ridicule which is so generally given them; as if they were the apes of Europeans, and their social state, arts, and government, the burlesques of the same things in Christendom. It may be excusable for the Chinese to have erroneous and contemptuous notions concerning lands and people of whom they have had little desire and less opportunity to learn what they really are; but such ideas entertained concerning them by those who have made greater attainments in morality, arts, and learning, greatly enfeebles the desire, and tends to excuse the duty, to impart these blessings to them. The names she has given her towns, the physiognomy God has marked upon the features of her people, the dress and fashions those people have chosen to adopt, their mechanical utensils, their religious festivals, their social usages; in short, almost every lineament of China and her inhabitants, has been the object of a laugh or the subject of a pun. Travellers who visit them are expected to give an account of

Mandarins with yellow buttons, handing you conserves of snails;
Smart young men about Canton in nankeen tights and peacocks'
    tails.
With many rare and dreadful dainties, kitten cutlets, puppy pies;

Birdsnest soup which (so convenient!) every bush around supplies.

Manners and customs, such as met the eye, and attracted attention by their newness and oddity, first found a place in their journals, and combined to continue the impression generally entertained, that the Chinese were on the whole an uninteresting, grotesque, and uncivilized 'pig-eyed' people, whom one run no risk in laughing at; an 'umbrella race', 'long-tailed celestials', at once conceited, ignorant, and almost unimprovable.

6) *The Chinese mind in a state of torpid hybernation*
(W. Gillespie, *The Land of Sinim*, pp. 27–9)
The conservative principle is strongly engraved on the Chinese mind. Change is abhorrent to them. They think it impossible to be wiser than their ancestors were thousands of years before them; and accordingly the first duty of a Chinese is to learn and revere the maxims of the sages, and to follow the customs of his forefathers. The result is that the Chinese mind is in a state of torpid hybernation. What one has said of Egypt may also be said of China – it is a petrifaction. The empire has long been in a state of stagnation. Their condition, both socially and intellectually, has been for centuries stationary ... Genius and originality are regarded as hostile and incompatible elements. ... Progress, in such a state of things, is impossible; and their present position, in respect of knowledge and civilization, is not only far behind that of the Western world, but in reality little in advance of what it was more than a thousand years ago ... [...]

Of late years, and since the termination of the British war, there has been a considerable degree of public spirit displayed by eminent citizens. There has also been a greater desire to adopt improvements from other nations than was probably ever before seen in their history. Still, however, they are slow to perceive, and reluctant to admit, their inferiority to foreigners in anything. If we must yield to the Chinese the name of being a civilized people, it is, after all, but a rude refinement and a barbarous civilization to which they have attained. If we compare them with the inhabitants of other countries, we must come to the conclusion, that ... they have not advanced and improved as they ought to have done.

7) *The impossibility of a Western mind forming a conception of Chinese character as a whole*
(G.W. Cooke, *China*, p. vii)

I have, in these letters, introduced no elaborate essay upon Chinese character. It is a great omission. No theme could be more tempting, no subject could afford wider scope for ingenious hypothesis, profound generalization, and triumphant dogmatism. Every small critic will, probably, utterly despise me for not having made something out of such opportunities. The truth is, that I have written several very fine characters for the whole Chinese race, but having the misfortune to have the people under my eye at the same time with my essay, they were always saying something or doing something which rubbed so rudely against my hypothesis, that in the interest of truth I burnt several successive letters. I may add that I have often talked over this matter with the most eminent and candid sinologues, and have always found them ready to agree with me as to the impossibility of a Western mind forming a conception of Chinese character as a whole. These difficulties, however, occur only to those who know the Chinese practically: a smart writer, entirely ignorant of the subject, might readily strike off a brilliant and antithetical analysis, which should leave nothing to be desired but Truth.

8) *An Operation*
(C. Toogood Downing, *The Fan-qui in China*, II, pp. 208–9)

On these trying occasions . . . many of the Chinese show the greatest fortitude. They have repaired to the operating-room with a firm and steady determination, when often their friends have been absorbed in grief without the room; thus showing that they have *moral*, if they are without *physical*, courage. They in general submit quietly, and require very little confinement by bandages or attendants. I assisted Dr. Parker one day, to extirpate a tumour, weighing nearly a pound, from the side of the neck of a female forty years of age. Although the operation required some minutes before it was completed, being situated . . . at the back of the jaw, the patient did not express the slightest impatience, and only once showed that she was sensible of the pain by drawing in the breath between her teeth.

This state of quietude under operations must not . . . be always attributed to fortitude in the patient, as in many cases there is present but a very slight degree of sensibility to suffering. There are many different degrees, no doubt, of this lethargic state of the body, but in general, I should think that it is in a ratio to the degree of cultivation of the mind of the individual. This subject deserves to be investigated; but at present we know that the savage American warrior smiles with disdain at the puny efforts of his enemies to torture his captive body, while the highly-polished European shrinks from the slightest touch, and feels uneasy and disturbed, if but a leaf be doubled under him as he lies upon his bed of roses.

9) *Cruelty and kindness among the Chinese*
(C.A. Gordon, *China, from a Medical Point of View*, p. 430)

From their earliest youth the Chinese are taught indifference to bodily suffering, or to life itself. Personal cruelty is instilled into their nature from their infancy; and so effectually, that I have seen by-standers and relations of a subject of operation smiling and joking as its details were being proceeded with, and I have seen a person just removed from the operating table ... smile at, and appear to enjoy the agonies of his successor, as the knife was cutting its way through, and the blood trickling from his quivering flesh.

And yet ... the Chinese are far from devoid of gratitude. Some have expressed themselves as deeply indebted to the foreign surgeons for having restored them in health to those dependent upon them for support; neither are they wanting in kindness and attention to each other during sickness. Brothers have been seen performing offices to one another, when prostrated by sickness, such as I must say I have never seen in what are called civilised countries. If therefore there are many objectionable points in the character of a Chinaman, even he has his redeeming ones.

10) *The Chinese nation much less vicious*
(D.F. Rennie, *Peking and the Pekingese*, I, pp. x–xi)

As far, however, as I have been able to judge, during two periods of service in China ... I have left the country with the conviction that the Chinese nation, as a whole, is a much less vicious one than, as a consequence of opinions formed from a limited and unfair field of observation, it has become customary to represent it; further, that the lower orders of the people generally are better conducted, more sober and industrious, and, taken altogether, intellectually superior to the corresponding classes of our own countrymen. This is an assertion I am quite prepared to have ridiculed, but I give it as my conviction, and I know it to be the conviction of many others of more extended experience, and better qualified for forming a judgment on such a question. Atrocities, frequently on a wholesale scale, occur in China, and so they do in all countries where bad characters and political discontent prevail; but because two or three hundred thousand of such men exist in a vast empire, that is no reason why upwards of four hundred millions of people should be viewed as equal to committing similar barbarities, any more than the atrocities committed during the Belfast riots of 1864 should be taken by the Chinese as illustrative of what the British people are. . . . If, therefore, a perusal of the following records should have the effect of placing the Chinese character, as represented by the Pekingese and the peasantry of Pa-chee-lee, in a more favourable light than any may have felt inclined to view it, I shall not feel that the time has been misapplied which I have spent on this work.

11) *The Renaissance in China*
(W.A.P. Martin, *The Chinese*, pp. 228–9)
As link after link is added to that chain of communication which brings China nearer to us than Europe was before the rise of steam navigation, it is interesting to know that a mental awakening is taking place among the people of China by which the Chinese mind will be brought proportionally nearer to our own.

The announcement of this fact will be received with distrust by some who are sceptical as to the doctrine of human progress. It will be questioned by others who deride as visionary the efforts of Christian enterprise. Nor will it be readily admitted by that large class who are wont to regard the Chinese mind as hopelessly incrusted with the prejudices of antiquity.

Never have a great people been more misunderstood. They are denounced as stolid, because we are not in possession of a medium sufficiently transparent to convey our ideas to them or transmit theirs to us; and stigmatized as barbarians, because we want the breadth to comprehend a civilization different from our own. They are represented as servile imitators, though they have borrowed less than any other people; as destitute of the inventive faculty, though the world is indebted to them for a long catalogue of the most useful discoveries; and as clinging with unquestioning tenacity to a heritage of traditions, though they have passed through many and profound changes in the course of their history.

12) *Vague and erroneous notions of China and the Chinese*
(W.H. Medhurst, *The Foreigner in Far Cathay*, pp. 1–2)
Everyone believes perhaps, and rightly, that China counts her population by hundreds of millions, and that her territory occupies a very considerable proportion of the Asiatic continent; and misty impressions are cherished no doubt as to the existence of evidences of an advanced state of civilization in the way of a literature, a philosophy, a highly-perfected social system, and so on. But test the information a little further, and it will be found that the prominent idea with regard to a Chinaman is that he is a quaint but stolid besotted creature, who smokes opium perpetually, and drowns his daughters as fast as they appear; whose every-day food consists of puppies, kittens, rats, and such like garbage; whose notions of honour, honesty, and courage, are of the loosest; and to whom cruelty is a pastime. This opinion may not quite tally with the impressions as to civilization and social advancement above alluded to, but no trouble is taken to explain the contradiction, and the more ridiculous and familiar fancy is indulged in.

13) *A weak and timid people*
(J.H. Gray, *China*, I, p. 15)
Of the moral character of the people . . . it is very difficult to speak justly. The moral character of the Chinese is a book written in strange letters, which are more complex and difficult for one of another race, religion, and language to decipher than their own singularly com-pounded word-symbols. In the same individual virtues and vices, apparently incompatible, are placed side by side. Meekness, gentleness, docility, industry, contentment, cheerfulness, obedience to superiors, dutifulness to parents, and reverence for the aged, are in one and the same person, the companions of insincerity, lying, flattery, treachery, cruelty, jealousy, ingratitude, avarice, and distrust of others. The Chinese are a weak and timid people, and in consequence, like all

146

similarly constituted races, they seek a natural refuge in deceit and fraud. But examples of moral inconsistency are by no means confined to the Chinese, and I fear that sometimes too much emphasis is laid on the dark side of their character . . .

14) *Vile and polluted in a shocking degree*
(S.W. Williams, *The Middle Kingdom*, revised edition, I, pp. 833–6)
In summing up the moral traits of Chinese character . . . we must necessarily compare them with that perfect standard given us from above. While their contrarieties indicate a different external civilization, a slight acquaintance with their morals proves their similarity to their fellow-men in the lineaments of a fallen and depraved nature. Some of the better traits of their character have been marvellously developed. They have attained, by the observance of peace and good order, to a high degree of security for life and property; the various classes of society are linked together in a remarkably homogeneous manner by the diffusion of education in the most moral books in their language and a general regard for the legal rights of property. Equality of competition for office removes the main incentive to violence in order to obtain posts of power and dignity, and industry receives its just reward of food, raiment, and shelter with a uniformity which encourages its constant exertion . . .

When, however, these traits have been mentioned, the Chinese are still more left without excuse for their wickedness, since being without law, they are a law unto themselves; they have always known better than they have done. With a general regard for outward decency, they are vile and polluted in a shocking degree; their conversation is full of filthy expressions and their lives of impure acts. They are somewhat restrained in the latter by the fences put around the family circle, so that seduction and adultery are comparatively infrequent, the former may even be said to be rare; but brothels and their inmates occur everywhere on land and on water . . .

More uneradicable than the sins of the flesh is the falsity of the Chinese, and its attendant sin of base ingratitude; their disregard of truth has perhaps done more to lower their character than any other fault. They feel no shame at being detected in a lie . . . nor do they fear any punishment from their gods for it. On the other hand, the necessity of the case compels them, in their daily intercourse with each other, to pay some regard to truth, and each man, from his own consciousness, knows just about how much to expect. Ambassadors and merchants have not been in the best position to ascertain their real character in this respect; for on the one side the courtiers of Peking thought themselves called upon by the mere presence of an embassy to put on some fictitious appearances, and on the other, the integrity and fair dealing of the hong merchants and great traders at Canton is in advance of the usual mercantile honesty of their countrymen. A Chinese requires but little motive to falsify, and he is constantly sharpening his wits to cozen his customer – wheedle him by promises and cheat him in goods or work. There is nothing which tries one so much when living among them as their disregard of truth, and renders him so indifferent as to what calamities may befall so mendacious a race. . . . Their better traits diminish in the distance, and patience is exhausted in its daily proximity and friction with this ancestor of all sins . . . [. . .]

On the whole, the Chinese present a singular mixture: if there is something to commend, there is more to blame; if they have some glaring vices, they have more virtues than most pagan nations. Ostentatious kindness and inbred suspicion, ceremonious civility and real rudeness, partial invention and servile imitation, industry and waste, sycophancy and self-dependence, are, with other dark and bright qualities, strangely blended. In trying to remedy the faults of their character by the restraints of law and the diffusion of education, they have no doubt hit upon the right mode; and their shortcomings show how ineffectual both must be until the Gospel comes to the aid of ruler and subject in elevating the moral sense of the whole nation. Female infanticide in some parts openly confessed, and divested of all disgrace and penalties everywhere; the dreadful prevalence of all the vices charged by the Apostle Paul upon the ancient heathen world; the alarming extent of the use of opium (furnished . . . by the power and skill of Great Britain from India), destroying the productions and natural resources of the people; the universal practice of lying and dishonest dealings; the unblushing lewdness of old and young; harsh cruelty toward prisoners by officers, and tyranny over slaves by masters – all form a full unchecked torrent of human depravity, and prove the existence of a kind and degree of moral degradation of which an excessive statement can scarcely be made, or an adequate conception hardly be formed.

15) *Chinese benevolence*
(A.H. Smith, *Chinese Characteristics*, pp. 190–1)
The same spirit is evinced in the curious ebullition of charitableness, which is known as the 'twelve eight gruel'. This performance may be regarded as a typical case of the most superficial form of Chinese benevolence. On the eighth day of the twelfth moon it is the custom for every one who has accumulated a quantity of benevolent impulses, which have had no opportunity for their gratification, to make the most liberal donations to all comers, of the very cheapest and poorest quality of soup, during about twelve hours of solar time. This is called 'practising virtue', and is considered to be a means of laying up merit. If the year happens to be one in which the harvest is bountiful, those who live in the country have perhaps no applicants for their coarse provender, as even the poorest people have as good or better at home. This circumstance does not, however, lead to the pretermission of the offer, much less to the substitution of anything of a better quality. On the contrary, the donors advertise their intentions with the same alacrity as in other years, not to say with greater, and when the day passes, and no one has asked for a single bowl of the rich gruel designed for them, it is merely put into the broken jars out of which the pigs are fed, and the wealthy man of practical benevolence retires to rest with the proud satisfaction that . . . he at least has done his duty for another year, and can in good conscience pose as a man of benevolence and virtue. But if, on the other hand, the year should be a bad one, and grain rises to a fabulous price, then this same man of means and of virtue fails to send out any notices of the 'practice of virtue' for this particular year, for the reason that he 'cannot afford it'!

16) *Moral bookkeeping*
(Isabella Bird, *The Yangtze Valley and Beyond*, p. 179)
Some writers, especially the author of *Chinese Characteristics*, while admitting the existence of charities on a large scale, detract from the admiration which such works of benevolence would naturally command by pointing out that they are regarded as 'practising virtue', and are considered to be a means of 'accumulating merit', and in fact that the object generally in view is 'not the benefit of the person on whom the "benevolence" terminates, but the extraction from the benefit conferred of a return benefit for the giver'. The Chinese are

perhaps the most practical people on earth, and a curious system of moral bookkeeping adopted by many shows this feature of the national character in a very curious light. There are books inculcating the practice of 'virtue', and in these a regular debtor and creditor account is opened, in which an individual charges himself with all his bad acts and credits himself with all his good ones, and the balance between the two exhibits his moral position at any given time.

Mr. Smith is a very acute observer, and has had lengthened opportunities of observation, and his conclusions as to the motives for benevolence must be received with respect. May it not, however, be hinted that an equally acute observer . . . after a residence of some years in England would consider himself warranted in referring a very considerable proportion of our benevolence to motives less worthy than the desire to 'accumulate merit'?

The problem of 'the poor and how to deal with them', has received, and is receiving, various solutions in China, and probably there is not a city without one or more organisations for the relief of permanent and special needs. Foundlings, orphans, blind persons, the aged, strangers, drowning persons, the destitute, the dead, and various other classes are objects of organised benevolence. The methods are not our methods, but they are none the less praiseworthy.

NOTE

1. Arthur H. Smith, *Chinese Characteristics*, revised edition (New York, 1894), p. 11.

GLOSSARY

AMOY   One of the ports opened by the Treaty of Nanking, 1842

ARROW   Ship flying the British flag seized by the Chinese on 8 October 1856 on suspicion of piracy. The incident led to the *Arrow* or Anglo-French War with China

AMUR, AMOOR   River forming the boundary between Manchuria and Russia

BABY TOWER   Brick receptacle for dead children too young to qualify for burial

BANNER TROOPS   Formations of Manchu soldiers (though there were also Mongol and Chinese banners)

BOAT-WOMAN   Woman of the Tanka or boat people of Canton

BONHAM, SIR GEORGE   Governor of Hong Kong, 1848–54. He visited the Taipings at Nanking in April 1853

BRAVE   Chinese soldier, who wore the character for 'brave' on his back

BRICK TEA   Common tea made into a brick-shaped slab used in Tibet and Mongolia

CANDAREEN   One-hundredth part of a Chinese ounce

CASH   Copper coin with a square hole in the middle, theoretically equal to one tael or Chinese ounce of silver

CATTY   Chinese pound, about 1⅓ lbs

CHAPOO, CHAPU   Port in Chekiang province seized by the British in 1842

CHEFOO (Chih-fu)   Treaty port in Shantung province

CHINA PROPER   Term referring to the eighteen provinces of China, that is the provinces south of the Great Wall and excluding Chinese central Asia

CHINKIANG (Chen-chiang)   City on the Yangtze opened by the treaty of Tientsin, 1858

CHRYSÊ   Border regions of Indo-China

CH'IEN-LUNG, KEENLUNG   Chinese emperor who reigned 1736–95

CHINA INLAND MISSION   Protestant missionary organization which sent its first missionaries to China in 1866

CHUNG WANG or Loyal King Li   Hsiu-ch'eng, the outstanding military leader of the later stages of the Taiping rebellion

CHUSAN   Island off the coast of Chekiang, occupied by the British in 1840

COMPRADOR   A Chinese handling the Chinese side of a foreign firm's business

ELGIN, THE EARL OF   British plenipotentiary at the time of the *Arrow* War

EVER-VICTORIOUS ARMY   European-officered Chinese force commanded by Charles Gordon in action against the Taipings

EXAMINATION HALL   Building used for the imperial examinations which gave successful candidates gentry status and qualified them for appointment as officials

EXTRATERRITORIALITY   Foreign legal jurisdiction over foreign nationals

FACTORY   Foreign trading settlement

FAN-QUI, FAN KWAE   Chinese term of abuse: 'foreign devil'

FENG-SHUI, 'wind and water'   Science or art of determining advantageous locations for buildings and graves

FLOWERY LAND   Translation of a Chinese term for China

FOO   Prefecture, sub-division of a province

FOOCHOW, FUHCHAU   Treaty port opened under the Treaty of Nanking, 1842; later the site of the Foochow Arsenal

FUTAI, FUT'AI   The Governor of a province

GENTRY   Term used for holders of official degrees

GINGAL, GINGALL   The Chinese blunderbuss

GINSENG   Medicinal plant, *panax repens*

GRAND CANAL   Water-way linking the Yangtze with north China.

HAN Synonym for China, referring to the Han dynasty, 202 BC–AD 220

HANKOW Treaty port on the Yangtze opened in 1858

HAN-LIN College in Peking to which the most successful scholars were appointed

HEAVENLY KING *See* Hung Saw-Chuen

HIEN (hsien) Administrative district

HONG MERCHANTS Chinese security merchants for foreign trade

HOPPO Chinese Superintendant of Customs at Canton

HO-SHEN Grand Secretary and notorious favourite of the Ch'ien-lung Emperor

HOUYHNMS Correctly Houyhnhnms: the noble and rational race of horses in Swift's *Gulliver's Travels*

HOWQUA, HOUQUA (Wu Ping-chien) Wealthiest of the Hong Merchants

HUNG SAW-CHUEN (Hung Hsiu-ch'üan) Leader of the Taiping Rebellion, who took the title of the T'ien Wang or Heavenly King

I, PRINCE OF *See* Kung, Prince

IMPERIAL MARITIME CUSTOMS Chinese customs service with a foreign inspectorate. Robert Hart became Inspector General in 1863

INTERPRETERS COLLEGE College established at Peking in 1862 to train language experts. W.A.P. Martin became president in 1869

JEHOL Emperor's summer residence in Manchuria

JU-EU-JOU (ju-i) Sceptre presented to signify that the recipient will attain his wishes

KOTOW Ceremony of prostration (three kneelings, nine head knockings) performed before the Emperor or his representative

KAN WANG Shield King, the Taiping leader Hung Jen-kan

KEENLONG *See* Ch'ien-lung

KEYING (Ch'i-ying) Manchu negotiator of the Treaty of Nanking and official responsible for the co-operative policy of the 1840s

KUNG, PRINCE Son of the Hsüan-tsung emperor. Chief negotiator of the Treaty of Tientsin and later in charge of the Tsungli Yamen

KWANGS   Two southern provinces of Kwangtung and Kwangsi

LI   A law

LI   Measure of distance, about ⅓ of a mile

LI HUNG-CHANG   Governor of Kiangsu province at the time of the Taiping rebellion. Later the leading Chinese statesman and proponent of 'self-strengthening'

LY (li)   Principle of rationalism

LITERATI   Alternative term for gentry

LEKIM, LIKIN (li-chin)   The 'tax of one-thousandth' first levied on goods in transit in 1853

LOLO   Non-Chinese group living in eastern Tibet

LOYAL KING   *See* Chung wang

MACE   One-tenth part of a Chinese ounce

MANCHUS, MANT-CHOW, MANTCHOO   Inhabitants of Manchuria who conquered China in the seventeenth century and founded the Manchu or Ch'ing dynasty

MAN-TSU, MAN-TZU   Non-Chinese people living in south-west China

MAOUTZE, MIAO-TZU   The Miao, a non-Chinese people living in south-west China

MARFOO   Groom

MINIÉ BALLS   Expanding bullets for the rifle invented by Claude Minié (1804–79)

MOORSOM   Shell with a percussion fuse invented by William Moorsom (1817–60)

MOSLEM REBELLION   Rebellion in Shensi and Kansu between 1862 and 1873

MOW (mou)   One sixth of an acre

NANKEEN   Cotton cloth from Nanking

NANKIN, NANKING   Southern capital, held by the Taipings from 1850 to 1864

NA WANG   Taiping leader Kao Yung-k'uan

NATURAL FOOT SOCIETY   Anti-footbinding society founded in 1895 by Mrs Archibald Little

NINGPO   Treaty port on the coast of Chekiang province
NORTHERN PRINCE   Taiping leader Wei Ch'ang-hui

ONE THOUSAND CHARACTER CLASSIC   Essay composed of one thousand different Chinese characters used in schools

PALANQUIN   Litter reserved for use by senior officials
PICUL   Malay word for a weight of 133⅓ lbs
PIDGIN-ENGLISH (pigeon English)   Originally, the language of communication used between English and Chinese on the China coast
PÊN-TS'AO (P'en-ts'ao kang-mu)   Chinese classic on materia medica, by Li Shih-chen (1518–93)

SAMSHU   Chinese rice spirit
SANGKOLINSIN (Seng-ko-lin-ch'in)   Mongol prince who fought the British and French in 1858–60
SELF-STRENGTHENING   Term used to denote the Chinese policy of selective adoption of western technology and institutions between 1860 and 1895
SHAMEEN   Artificial island occupied by the foreign settlement in Canton
SHING   Chinese measure of about one pint
SIEN SHENG (hsien-sheng)   Chinese term for Mr or teacher
SINIM   Biblical place name believed to refer to China
SOOCHOW, SÜCHOW (Su-chou)   City in Kiangsu province
SOWAR   Trooper in the Indian army
SYCEE   Silver ingots

TAEL   Ounce of silver, a measure but not a coin. For most of the nineteenth century this exchanged at three taels to the £1 sterling, or one tael for US $1.63
TAI-PING 'Heavenly Peace'   Name given to the rebellion which engulfed central China between 1850 and 1864
TAKU FORTS   Forts guarding the entrance to the Peiho or northern river
TAOISM, TAÔISM   Chinese philosophy and religion traced back to Lao-tzu, said to have been born in 604 BC

TAOU-SZE Taoist priest

TARTAR Term denoting peoples of Central Asia, including the Manchus

TA TSING LEU LI (Ta Ch'ing Lü Li) Codified laws and statutes of the Ch'ing dynasty, 1644–1911

TEA STONE Variety of rose quartz used to make the lenses of spectacles

TIENTSIN, TEIN-TSIN Port opened by the Treaty of Tientsin, 1858, which also opened the Yangtze to foreign navigation

TIEN-WANG *See* Hung Saw-Chuen

TIRAILLEURS French sharp-shooters

TOU A peck or two gallons

TRACKER One who tows a vessel

TREATY PORTS Ports opened to foreign trade and residence under the unequal treaties

TRIBUTE Gifts offered to the Emperor by representatives of nations on China's periphery, which symbolized recognition that China was a superior state

TRIPITAKA Chinese Buddhist canonical writings

TSUNG-LI YAMUN colloquially 'the Yamen'. Prototype Chinese Foreign Office, established in 1861

UNEQUAL TREATIES Treaties signed between China and the West by which China surrendered control over tariffs and jurisdiction over foreigners

VICEROY Term used to refer to the Governor-General of one or more provinces

WANG King, title taken by the Taiping leaders

WHAMPOA Anchorage on the Pearl River south of Canton

WHEATON Henry Wheaton, author of *Elements of International Law*

WRITER Clerk in the service of the Imperial Maritime Customs

YAMEN, YAMUN Office and residence of an official

YANG-JEN Chinese term for a foreigner

YEH MING-CH'EN Viceroy of Kwangtung and Kwangsi at the

time of the *Arrow* war. After the capture of Canton he was sent to Calcutta, where he died

YIN AND YANG   Female and male principles

YÜAN-MING-YÜAN   Summer residence of the emperors, about nine miles from Peking

YÜAN SHIH-K'AI   Prominent official of the late imperial period and creator of the Peiyang army, China's first modern military force. After the 1911 Revolution he became President of the Republic

ZENDAVESTA   Ancient writings of the Parsees

BIBLIOGRAPHY

The place of publication is London unless otherwise stated.

CONTEMPORARY SOURCES

'Agriculture in China', *Chinese Repository*, 3, 1834, pp. 121–7.
Alabaster, Ernest, *Notes and Commentaries on Chinese Criminal Law and Cognate Topics: With Special Relation to Ruling Cases, together with a Brief Excursus on the Law of Property, Chiefly founded on the Writings of the Late Sir Chaloner Alabaster, K.C.M.G.*, 1899.
Alcock, Rutherford, 'The Chinese Empire and its destinies', *Bombay Quarterly Review*, 4, October, 1855, pp. 219–250.
Atkinson, Thomas Witlam, *Travels in the Regions of the Upper and Lower Amoor and the Russian Acquisitions on the Confines of India and China: With Adventures among the Mountain Kirghis; and the Manjours, Manyargs, Toungouz, Touzemtz, Goldi, and Gelyaks: the Hunting and Pastoral Tribes*, 1860.
Baber, E. Colborne, 'Travels and researches in Western China', *Royal Geographical Society Supplementary Papers*, vol. I, part I, 1882.
Barrow, John, *Travels in China: Containing Descriptions, Observations, and Comparisons, Made and Collected in the Course of a Short Residence at the Imperial Palace of Yuen-Min-Yuen, and on a Subsequent Journey through the Country from Peking to Canton. In which it is Attempted to Appreciate the Rank that this Extraordinary Empire may be Considered to Hold in the Scale of Civilized Nations*, second edition, 1806; Taipei, 1972.
Beal, S., *Buddhism in China*, 1884.
Beresford, Lord Charles, *The Break-up of China: With an Account of Its Present Commerce, Currency, Waterways, Armies, Railways, Politics and Future Prospects*, 1899.
Bernard, W.D., *The Nemesis in China: Comprising a History of the Late*

War in that Country; with an Account of the Colony of Hong-Kong. From the Notes of Captain W.H. Hall, R.N. and Personal Observations by W.D. Bernard, Esq. A.M. Oxon, third edition, 1847; San Francisco, 1974.

Bird, Isabella, *The Yangtze Valley and Beyond: An Account of Journeys in China, Chiefly in the Province of Sze Chuan and among the Man-tze of the Somo Territory*, 1899; 1985.

Blakiston, Thomas W., *Five Months on the Yang-tsze: With a Narrative of the Exploration of Its Upper Waters, and Notices of the Present Rebellion in China*, 1862.

Bretschneider, E., 'The study and value of Chinese botanical works', *Chinese Recorder*, 3, 1870, pp. 157–63.

Bryson, Mrs (Mary Isabella), *Child Life in China*.

Bryson, Mrs (Mary Isabella), *John Kenneth Mackenzie: Medical Missionary to China*, 1891.

Callery, (Joseph) and Yvan, *History of the Insurrection in China. With Notices of the Christianity, Creed, and Proclamations of the Insurgents*, trans. John Oxenford, 1853; New York, 1969.

Cavendish, Major A.E.J., 'The armed strength (?) of China', *Journal of the United Service Institution*, 42, 1898, pp. 705–23.

Chinese Repository, 20 vols., Canton, 1833–51; reprint of second edition, Tokyo, 1965.

Clark, Ellis, 'Notes on the Progress of Mining in China', *Transactions of the American Institute of Mining Engineers*, 19, 1890–1, pp. 571–95.

Cobbold, Revd R.H., *Pictures of the Chinese, Drawn by Themselves*, 1860.

Colquhoun, Archibald R., *Across Chrysê: Being the Narrative of a Journey of Exploration through the South China Border Lands from Canton to Mandalay*, 2 vols., third edition, 1883.

Colquhoun, Archibald R., *China in Transformation*, 1898.

Cooke, George Wingrove, *China: Being* The Times *Special Correspondence from China in the Years 1857–58*, 1858.

Cooper, T.T., *Travels of Pioneer of Commerce in Pigtail and Petticoats; or, An Overland Journey from China Towards India*, 1871.

Culbertson, Revd M. Simpson, *Darkness in the Flowery Land; or Religious Notions and Popular Superstitions in North China*, New York, 1857.

Curzon, The Hon. George N., MP, *Problems of the Far East*, 1894.

Davis, John Francis, *Poeseos Sinensis Commentarii: On the Poetry of the Chinese, (from the Royal Asiatic Transactions) to Which are added Translations and Detached Pieces*, Macao, 1834.

Davis, John Francis, *The Chinese: A General Description of the Empire of China and its Inhabitants*, 2 vols., New York, 1836; Wilmington, 1972.

Davis, Sir John Francis, *China: During the War and Since the Peace*, 2 vols., 1852; Wilmington, 1972.

Davis, Sir John Francis, *Chinese Miscellanies: A Collection of Essays and Notes*, 1865.

Doolittle, Revd Justus, *Social Life of the Chinese: With Some Account of Their Religious, Governmental, Educational, and Business Customs and Opinions, with Special but not Exclusive Reference to Fuhchau*, 2 vols., New York, 1865; Taipei, 1966.

Douglas, Robert K., *The Language and Literature of China: Two Lectures Delivered at the Royal Institution of Great Britain in May and June, 1875*, 1875.

Downing, C. Toogood, *The Fan-qui in China in 1836–7*, 3 vols., 1838; Shannon, 1972.

Drage, Charles, *Servants of the Dragon Throne: Being the Lives of Edward and Cecil Bowra*, 1966.

Du Halde, Jean-Baptiste, *A Description of the Empire of China and Chinese-Tartary Together with the Kingdoms of Korea, and Tibet: Containing the Geography and History (Natural as well as Civil) of those Countries*, 2 vols., 1738, 1741.

Edkins, Jane R., *Chinese Scenes and People: With Notices of Christian Missions and Missionary Life in a Series of Letters from Various Parts of China; With a Narrative of a Visit to Nanking by Her Husband the Rev. Joseph Edkins B.A.*, 1863.

Edkins, Joseph, *The Religious Condition of the Chinese: With Observations on the Prospects of Christian Conversion amongst that People*, 1859; Taipei, 1974.

Eitel, Revd E.J., *Feng-shui; or The Rudiments of Natural Science in China*, Hong Kong, 1873, third edition of reprint, Bath, 1979.

Eitel, Revd E.J., 'Amateur Sinology', *China Review*, 2, 1873, pp. 1–8.

Elgin, Eighth Earl of, *Extracts from the Letters of James Earl of Elgin etc. etc. to Mary Louisa Countess of Elgin 1847–1862*, 1864.

Elgin, Eighth Earl of, *Letters and Journals of James, Eighth Earl of Elgin,* ed. Theodore Walrond, 1872.

Ellis, Henry, *Journal of the Proceedings of the Late Embassy to China: Comprising a Correct Narrative of the Public Transactions of the Embassy, of the Voyage to and from China, and of the Journey from the Mouth of the Pei-ho to the Return to Canton. Interspersed with Observations upon the Face of the Country, the Polity, Moral Character, and Manners of the Chinese Nation*, 1817.

Field, Henry M., *From Egypt to Japan*, sixteenth edition, New York, 1890.

Fishbourne, Captain E.G., *Impressions of China, and the Present Revolution: Its Progress and Prospects*, 1855.

Fisher, Lt.-Col. (Arthur a'Court), *Personal Narrative of Three Years' Service in China*, 1863.

Fortune, Robert, *A Journey to the Tea Countries of China; Including Sung-lo and the Bohea Hills; With a Short Notice of the East India Company's Tea Plantations in the Himalaya Mountains*, 1852; 1987.

Giles, Herbert A., *An Introduction to the History of Chinese Pictorial Art*, Shanghai, 1905; second edition, Shanghai, 1918.

Gillespie, William, *The Land of Sinim; or, China and Chinese Missions*, Edinburgh, 1854.

Giquel, Prosper, trans. H. Lang, *The Foochow Arsenal, and Its Results: From the Commencement in 1867, to the End of the Foreign Directorate, on the 16th February, 1874*, Shanghai, 1874.

Gordon, Charles Alexander, *China from a Medical Point of View in 1860 and 1861: To Which is Added a Chapter on Nagasaki as a Sanitarium*, 1863.

Gray, The Venerable John Henry, *Walks in the City of Canton*, Hong Kong, 1875; San Francisco, 1974.

Gray, John Henry, *China: A History of the Laws, Manners, and Customs of the People*, 2 vols, 1878; Shannon, 1972.

Guinness, M. Geraldine, *The Story of the China Inland Mission, with an Introduction by J. Hudson Taylor*, 2 vols., 1893.

Gutzlaff, Charles, *Journal of Three Voyages along the Coast of China in 1831, 1832, & 1833, with Notices of Siam, Corea, and the Loo-choo Islands: To Which is Prefixed an Introductory Essay on the Policy, Religion, etc. of China, by the Rev. W. Ellis*, 1834; Taipei, 1968.

Hart, Robert, *Entering China's Service: Robert Hart's Journals, 1854–1863*, ed. K.F. Bruner, J.K. Fairbank and R.J. Smith, 1986.

Hosie, Alexander, *Three Years in Western China: A Narrative of Three Journeys in Ssŭ-ch'uan, Kuei-chow, and Yün-nan,* 1890.

Huc, M. (Évariste), *The Chinese Empire: Forming a Sequel to the Work Entitled 'Recollections of a Journey Through Tartary and Thibet.',* 2 vols., second edition, 1855; New York, 1970.

Hunter, W.C., *The 'Fan Kwae' at Canton Before Treaty Days 1825–1844,* 1882; Taipei, 1970.

'Illustrations of men and things in China: priest collecting paper; uses of blood; mode of cutting glass; a 'Chinaman', *Chinese Repository,* 10, 1841, pp. 104–8.

Jamieson, George, 'Tenure of land in China and the condition of the rural population', *Journal of the North China Branch of the Royal Asiatic Society,* new series, 23, no. 6, 1889, pp. 59–117.

Jones, Owen, *The Grammar of Ornament: Illustrated by Examples from Various Styles of Ornament,* 1856.

Lamprey, J., 'The Economy of the Chinese Army', *Journal of the Royal United Service Institution,* 11, no. 46, 1867, pp. 403–433.

Lane-Poole, Stanley, *Sir Harry Parkes in China,* 1901, Taipei, 1968.

Legge, James, trans., *The Chinese Classics,* 8 vols., second edition, Oxford, 1893; vol I reprinted as *Confucius: Confucian Analects, The Great Learning, and The Doctrine of the Mean,* New York, 1971.

Lindley, Augustus F. (Lin-le), *Ti-ping Tien-kwoh: The History of The Tai-ping Revolution: Including a Narrative of the Author's Personal Adventures,* 2 vols., 1866; 2 vols. in one, New York, 1970.

Little, Mrs Archibald, (Alicia Bewicke), *The Land of the Blue Gown,* 1902.

Macartney, Lord, *An Embassy to China: Being the Journal Kept by Lord Macartney during his Embassy to The Emperor Ch'ien-lung 1793–1794,* ed. J.L. Cranmer-Byng, 1962.

MacFarlane, Charles, *The Chinese Revolution: With Details of the Habits, Manners, and Customs of China and the Chinese,* 1853; Wilmington, 1972.

Mackie, J. Milton, *Life of Tai-ping-wang, Chief of the Chinese Insurrection,* New York, 1857; San Francisco, 1978.

Martin, W.A.P., *The Chinese: Their Education, Philosophy, and Letters,* 1881.

Martin, W.A.P., *A Cycle of Cathay; or, China, South and North with Personal Reminiscences,* New York, 1900; Taipei, 1966.

Mayers, William Frederick, *The Chinese Reader's Manual: A Handbook of Biographical, Historical, Mythological, and General Literary Reference*, Shanghai, 1874; Taipei, 1964.

Meadows, Thomas Taylor, *Desultory Notes on the Government and People of China, and on the Chinese Language: Illustrated with a Sketch of the Province of Kwang-tûng, Showing Its Division into Departments and Districts*, 1847.

Meadows, Thomas Taylor, *The Chinese and Their Rebellions: Viewed in Connection with Their National Philosophy, Ethics, Legislation, and Administration. To Which is Added, an Essay on Civilization and Its Present State in the East and West*, 1856; Shannon, 1972.

Medhurst, [Dr] W.H., *China: Its State and Prospects, with Especial Reference to the Spread of the Gospel: Containing Allusions to the Antiquity, Extent, Population, Civilization, Literature, and Religion of the Chinese*, 1838; Wilmington, 1973.

Medhurst, W.H., *The Foreigner in Far Cathay*, 1872.

M'Ghee, Revd R.J.L., *How We Got to Pekin: A Narrative of the Campaign in China of 1860*, 1862.

Michie, Alexander, *The Englishman in China During the Victorian Era: As Illustrated in the Career of Sir Rutherford Alcock, K.C.B., D.C.L.*, 2 vols., Edinburgh, 1900; Taipei, 1966.

Milne, William C., *Life in China*, new edition, 1859.

Moges, The Marquis de, *Recollections of Baron Gros's Embassy to China and Japan in 1857–58*, 1860; Shannon, 1972.

Morse, Hosea Ballou, *The International Relations of the Chinese Empire*, 3 vols., 1910–18; Taipei, 1963.

Nevius, Revd John L., *China and the Chinese: A General Description of the Country and Its Inhabitants; Its Civilization and Form of Government; Its Religion and Social Institutions; Its Intercourse with Other Nations; and Its Present Condition and Prospects*, New York, 1869.

North China Herald, Shanghai, 1850–67.

Oliphant, Laurence, *Narrative of the Earl of Elgin's Mission to China and Japan in the Years 1857, '58, '59*, 2 vols., 1859; 1970.

Ouchterlony, Lieutenant John, *The Chinese War: An Account of All the Operations of the British Forces from the Commencement to the Treaty of Nanking*, 1844.

'Philosinensis' [C. Gutzlaff], 'Remarks on the history and chronology of China, from the earliest ages down to the present time', *Chinese Repository*, 2, 1833–4, pp. 74–85.

'Philosinensis' [C. Gutzlaff], 'Remarks on Budhism; together with brief notices of the island of Poo-to, and of the numerous priests who inhabit it'. *Chinese Repository*, 2, 1833–4, pp. 214–225.

Pumpelly, Raphael, 'A journey in northern China', *Galaxy*, 8, 1869, pp. 467–76.

Rennie, D.F., *Peking and the Pekingese during the First Year of the British Embassy at Peking*, 2 vols., 1865.

Roberts, Issachar J., Letter to the editor, *Chinese and General Missionary Gleaner*, February, 1853.

Scarth, J.R., *Twelve Years in China: The People, the Rebels, and the Mandarins*, Edinburgh, 1860; Wilmington, 1972.

Scott, J. George, 'The Chinese Brave', *Asiatic Quarterly Review*, 1, 1886, pp. 222–45.

Sirr, Henry Charles, *China and the Chinese: Their Religion, Character, Customs, and Manufactures; the Evils Arising from the Opium Trade; with a Glance at Our Religious, Moral, Political, and Commercial Intercourse with the Country*, 2 vols., 1849; San Francisco, 1978.

Smith, Arthur H., *Chinese Characteristics*, revised edition, New York, 1894.

Swinhoe, Robert, *Narrative of the North China Campaign of 1860: Containing Personal Experiences of Chinese Character, and of the Moral and Social Condition of the Country; Together with a Description of the Interior of Pekin*, 1861.

'Ta Tsing Leu Lee; being the fundamental Laws, and a Selection from the supplementary Statutes, of the Penal Code of China. . . . By Sir George Thomas Staunton, Bart. . . . London, 1810', *Edinburgh Review*, 16, 1810, pp. 476–99.

Williams, S. Wells, *The Middle Kingdom: A Survey of the Geography, Government, Education, Social Life, Arts, Religion, &c., of the Chinese Empire and its Inhabitants*, 2 vols., fourth edition, New York, 1861. Revised edition, *The Middle Kingdom: A Survey of the Geography, Government, Literature, Social Life, Arts, and History of the Chinese Empire and Its Inhabitants*, 2 vols., New York, 1883; Taipei, 1965.

Williamson, Revd Alexander, *Journeys in North China, Manchuria, and Eastern Mongolia; With Some Account of Korea*, 2 vols., 1870.

Wilson, Andrew, *The 'Ever-Victorious Army': A History of the Chinese*

Campaign under Lt.-Col. C.G. Gordon, C.B. R.E. and of the Suppression of the Tai-ping Rebellion, Edinburgh, 1868; San Francisco, 1977.

Wolseley, Lieut.-Colonel G.J., *Narrative of the War with China in 1860: To Which is Added the Account of a Short Residence with the Tai-ping Rebels at Nankin and a Voyage from Thence to Hankow*, 1862; Wilmington, 1972.

British Parliamentary Papers

Papers Respecting the Civil War in China, 1853; Shannon, 1971.
Correspondence with the Superintendent of British Trade in China, upon the Subject of Emigration from that Country, 1853; Shannon, 1971.
Commercial Reports by Her Majesty's Consuls in China: 1877, 1878; Shannon, 1971.

GENERAL WORKS

Cameron, Nigel, *Barbarians and Mandarins: Thirteen Centuries of Western Travelers in China*, New York, 1970.

Clarke, Prescott and Gregory, J.S., *Western Reports on the Taiping*, Honolulu, 1982.

Coates, P.D., *The China Consuls: British Consular Officers, 1843–1943*, Oxford, 1988.

Cordier, Henri, *Bibliotheca Sinica: Dictionnaire bibliographique des ouvrages relatifs à l'empire chinois*, 5 vols., Paris, 1904–24.

Dawson, Raymond, *The Chinese Chameleon: An Analysis of European Concepts of Chinese Civilization*, 1967.

Kiernan, V.G., *The Lords of Human Kind: European Attitudes to the Outside World in the Imperial Age*, 1969; 1972.

Mackerras, Colin, *Western Images of China*, Hong Kong, 1989.

Mason, Mary Gertrude, *Western Concepts of China and the Chinese, 1840–1876*, New York, 1939.

ACKNOWLEDGEMENTS

I must thank my colleagues at the Polytechnic of Huddersfield, and especially Keith Dockray, for encouragement in producing this Reader. It had its origins in a course on the history of China in the nineteenth and twentieth centuries which I have long given to final-year students. I hope that the selection of readings which I have put together here will amuse, horrify and perhaps enlighten them and their successors.

I must offer particular thanks to the Polytechnic Library staff, who have patiently assisted in obtaining the many books and articles on which the Reader is based. I have a large debt of gratitude to my wife, Jan, for proof-reading.

The author and publisher wish to apologize for any inadvertent infringement of copyright.